Hands-On Reactive Programming with Reactor

Build reactive and scalable microservices using the Reactor framework

Rahul Sharma

BIRMINGHAM - MUMBAI

Hands-On Reactive Programming with Reactor

Commissioning Editor: Aaron Lazar
Acquisition Editor: Denim Pinto
Content Development Editor: Tiksha Sarang
Technical Editor: Abhishek Sharma
Copy Editor: Safis Editing
Project Coordinator: Prajakta Naik
Proofreader: Safis Editing
Indexer: Pratik Shirodkar
Graphics: Jisha Chirayil
Production Coordinator: Shantanu Zagade

First published: September 2018

Production reference: 1280918

Published by Packt Publishing Ltd.
Livery Place
35 Livery Street
Birmingham
B3 2PB, UK.

ISBN 978-1-78913-579-4

www.packtpub.com

`mapt.io`

Mapt is an online digital library that gives you full access to over 5,000 books and videos, as well as industry leading tools to help you plan your personal development and advance your career. For more information, please visit our website.

Why subscribe?

- Spend less time learning and more time coding with practical eBooks and videos from over 4,000 industry professionals

- Improve your learning with Skill Plans built especially for you

- Get a free eBook or video every month

- Mapt is fully searchable

- Copy and paste, print, and bookmark content

Packt.com

Did you know that Packt offers eBook versions of every book published, with PDF and ePub files available? You can upgrade to the eBook version at `www.Packt.com` and as a print book customer, you are entitled to a discount on the eBook copy. Get in touch with us at `customercare@packtpub.com` for more details.

At `www.Packt.com`, you can also read a collection of free technical articles, sign up for a range of free newsletters, and receive exclusive discounts and offers on Packt books and eBooks.

Contributors

About the author

Rahul Sharma is a seasoned Java developer with around 13 years' experience in Java/J2EE applications. He has worked at companies ranging from enterprises to start-ups. Being an open source enthusiast, he has contributed to various projects, including Apache Crunch. He is currently working with a Java framework, Project Reactor.

About the reviewer

Suchit Khanna is a seasoned developer, cricket enthusiast, and an avid traveler. He has worked for more than a decade in helping to build maintainable and scalable enterprise systems. When he's not writing code, he's most likely playing cricket or traveling with his better half.

Packt is searching for authors like you

If you're interested in becoming an author for Packt, please visit `authors.packtpub.com` and apply today. We have worked with thousands of developers and tech professionals, just like you, to help them share their insight with the global tech community. You can make a general application, apply for a specific hot topic that we are recruiting an author for, or submit your own idea.

Table of Contents

Preface

Reactor is an implementation of the Java 9 Reactive Streams specification, an API for asynchronous data processing. This specification is based on a reactive programming paradigm, enabling developers to build enterprise-grade, robust applications with reduced complexity and in less time. *Hands-On Reactive Programming with Reactor* shows you how Reactor works, as well as how to use it to develop reactive applications in Java.

The book begins with the fundamentals of Reactor and the role it plays in building effective applications. You will learn how to build fully non-blocking applications and will later be guided on the Publisher and Subscriber APIs. The first four chapters will help you to understand Reactive Streams and the Reactor framework. The following four chapters use Reactor to build a microservices SpringWebFlux extension to build REST-based web services. They demonstrate the concepts of the flow, backpressure, and execution models. You will gain an understanding of how to use two reactive composable APIs, Flux and Mono, which are used extensively to implement Reactive Extensions. In the final two chapters, you will gain an understanding of Reactive Streams and the Reactor framework.

The chapters explain the most important parts and build simple programs to establish a foundation. By the end of the book, you will have gained enough confidence to build reactive and scalable microservices.

Who this book is for

For anyone with a basic understanding of Java's fundamental concepts, and how to develop event-driven and data-driven applications easily with Reactor, this book is for you – a step-by-step guide to getting you up and running with Reactive Streams and the Reactor framework.

What this book covers

Chapter 1, *Getting Started with Reactive Streams*, explains the Reactive Streams API and introduces the reactive paradigm and its benefits. The chapter also introduces Reactor as an implementation of Reactive Streams.

Chapter 2, *The Publisher and Subscriber APIs in a Reactor*, explains the Producer and Subscriber APIs and the corresponding Flux and Mono implications of Reactor. It also discusses use cases of Flux and Mono and the respective Sinks. We will also look into Hot and Cold variants of the components.

Chapter 3, *Data and Stream Processing*, tackles how we can process data generated by a Publisher before it gets consumed by a Subscriber, the possible operations available, and combining them to build a robust stream-processing pipeline. Stream processing also involves converting, pivoting, and aggregating data, and then generating new data.

Chapter 4, *Processors*, introduces the out-of-the-box processors available in Reactor. Processors are special Publishers, which are also Subscribers, and it is quite important to understand why we need them before jumping into putting one into practice.

Chapter 5, *SpringWebFlux for Microservices*, introduces SpringWebFlux, a Reactor web extension. It explains the concepts of the RouterFunction, HandlerFunction, and FilterFunction. We will then build a REST-based microservice using Mongo as a store.

Chapter 6, *Dynamic Rendering*, integrates a templating engine into the REST-based microservice we introduced in the previous chapter, to render dynamic content. It also demonstrates request filters.

Chapter 7, *Flow Control and Backpressure*, discusses flow control, an important aspect of reactive programming, which is essentially required to control overruns by a fast Publisher. It also discusses various ways to control the complete pipeline processing.

Chapter 8, *Handling Errors*, as its title suggests, explains how to handle errors. All Java developers are accustomed to the try-catch-finally block of error handling. This chapter translates it for stream processing. It also covers how we can recover from an error and how can we go about generating errors. This is an essential requirement for all enterprise applications.

Chapter 9, *Execution Control*, looks at the various strategies available in Reactor for processing the built stream. It could be scheduled at some interval or batched in groups, or all operations can be performed in parallel.

Chapter 10, *Testing and Debugging*, lists ways we can test a stream, because no development is complete without being tested. We will build JUnit tests that will use some of the testing utilities offered by Reactor to create robust tests. The chapter also lists ways to go about debugging asynchronous flows built over Reactor.

To get the most out of this book

- It is essential to have a sound understanding of the basic Java concepts
- Java Standard Edition, JDK 8, and IntelliJ IDEA IDE or above are required

Download the example code files

You can download the example code files for this book from your account at www.packt.com. If you purchased this book elsewhere, you can visit www.packt.com/support and register to have the files emailed directly to you.

You can download the code files by following these steps:

1. Log in or register at www.packt.com.
2. Select the **SUPPORT** tab.
3. Click on **Code Downloads & Errata**.
4. Enter the name of the book in the **Search** box and follow the onscreen instructions.

Once the file is downloaded, please make sure that you unzip or extract the folder using the latest version of:

- WinRAR/7-Zip for Windows
- Zipeg/iZip/UnRarX for Mac
- 7-Zip/PeaZip for Linux

The code bundle for the book is also hosted on GitHub at https://github.com/PacktPublishing/Hands-On-Reactive-Programming-with-Reactor. In case there's an update to the code, it will be updated on the existing GitHub repository.

We also have other code bundles from our rich catalog of books and videos available at https://github.com/PacktPublishing/. Check them out!

Conventions used

There are a number of text conventions used throughout this book.

`CodeInText`: Indicates code words in text, database table names, folder names, filenames, file extensions, pathnames, dummy URLs, user input, and Twitter handles. Here is an example: "All `Subscribe` methods return a `Disposable` type. This type can also be used to cancel the subscription."

A block of code is set as follows:

```
public interface Publisher<T> {
    public void subscribe(Subscriber<? super T> s);
}
```

Any command-line input or output is written as follows:

```
gradlew bootrun
```

Bold: Indicates a new term, an important word, or words that you see onscreen.

 Warnings or important notes appear like this.

 Tips and tricks appear like this.

Get in touch

Feedback from our readers is always welcome.

General feedback: If you have questions about any aspect of this book, mention the book title in the subject of your message and email us at `customercare@packtpub.com`.

Errata: Although we have taken every care to ensure the accuracy of our content, mistakes do happen. If you have found a mistake in this book, we would be grateful if you would report this to us. Please visit `www.packt.com/submit-errata`, selecting your book, clicking on the Errata Submission Form link, and entering the details.

Piracy: If you come across any illegal copies of our works in any form on the Internet, we would be grateful if you would provide us with the location address or website name. Please contact us at `copyright@packt.com` with a link to the material.

If you are interested in becoming an author: If there is a topic that you have expertise in and you are interested in either writing or contributing to a book, please visit `authors.packtpub.com`.

Reviews

Please leave a review. Once you have read and used this book, why not leave a review on the site that you purchased it from? Potential readers can then see and use your unbiased opinion to make purchase decisions, we at Packt can understand what you think about our products, and our authors can see your feedback on their book. Thank you!

For more information about Packt, please visit `packt.com`.

Getting Started with Reactive Streams

1

Over the years, application architecture has evolved. Businesses increasingly need to build systems that remain responsive and can scale when required. Systems should also be maintainable and quickly releasable. In accordance with these needs, we have started to build applications as loosely coupled services. We no longer build a system as one big application. Instead, we split systems into multiple independent, autonomous services. The objective for such services is to do one thing, and do it well.

In this chapter, we will discuss concerns associated with building such services. We will also look at how to address those concerns.

Technical requirements

- Java Standard Edition, JDK 8 or above
- IntelliJ IDEA IDE, 2018.1 or above

The GitHub link for this chapter is `https://github.com/PacktPublishing/Hands-On-Reactive-Programming-with-Reactor/tree/master/Chapter01`.

Reactive architecture

When we start to build microservice architecture, we try to involve different services to deliver business solutions. We often build services as traditional API models, where each of the services can interact with other services. This is referred to as **distributed architecture**. If a distributed architecture is designed incorrectly, performance issues surface very quickly. It can be difficult to have numerous distributed services that work concurrently to deliver the intended performance. Companies that offer services requiring large data exchange (such as Netflix, Amazon, or Lightbend) have therefore seen a need for alternative paradigms, which can be used for systems with the following characteristics:

- Consisting of very loosely coupled components
- Responding to user inputs
- Resilient to varying load conditions
- Always available

In order to achieve the preceding characteristics, we need to build event-driven, modular services that communicate with each other by using notifications. In turn, we can respond to the system's flow of events. The modular services are more scalable, as we can add or remove service instances without halting the complete application. The complete architecture will be fault tolerant if we can isolate errors and take corrective actions. The preceding four characteristics are the basic principles of the **Reactive Manifesto**. The Reactive Manifesto states that each reactive system should consist of loosely coupled components that rely on asynchronous, message-driven architecture. They must remain responsive to user input and isolate failures to individual components. Replication must be done in order to respond to varying load conditions. The following is a diagram of the Reactive Manifesto:

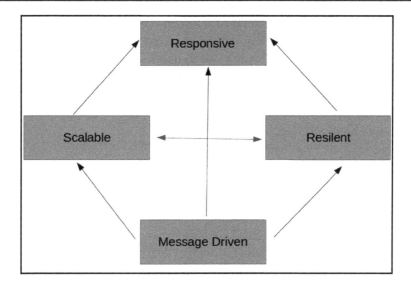

The Reactive Manifesto describes a reactive system. It does not required that the system be based on reactive programming, or any other reactive library. We can build a message-driven, resilient, scalable, and responsive application without using a reactive library, but it is easier to build an application based on reactive libraries.

Reactive programming

Most of us write imperative applications, where statements are required in order to change the application state. The code is executed and a final state is arrived at. After the state's computation, the state does not change when the underlying factors do. Let's consider the following code as an example:

```
int value1 = 5;
int value2 = 10;
int sum = val1 + val2;
System.out.println(sum); // 15
value1 = 15;
System.out.println(sum); // 15
```

The sum is still 15, even though value1 has been changed.

On the other hand, reactive programming is about the propagation of change. It is also referred to as **declarative programming**, where we express our intent and application state as dynamically determined by changes to underlying factors. The preceding sum program example, under a reactive paradigm, would behave as follows:

```
int value1 = 5;
int value2 = 10;
int sum = val1 + val2;
System.out.println(sum); // 15
value1 = 15;
System.out.println(sum); // 25
```

Consequently, if a program reacts to changes in the underlying factors, it can be called reactive. Reactive programs can be built using imperative techniques, like callbacks. This may be fine for a program that has a single event. However, for applications where hundreds of events are happening, this could easily lead to callback hell; we could have numerous callbacks relying on one another, and it would be really difficult to figure out which ones were being executed. As a result, we require a new set of abstractions that enable us to seamlessly build asynchronous, event-driven interactions across a network boundary. There are libraries in different imperative languages, like Java, that provide us with these abstractions. These libraries are referred to as **Reactive Extensions**.

ReactiveX

Reactive Extensions, also known as ReactiveX, enable us to express the asynchronous events in an application as a set of observable sequences. Other applications can subscribe to these observables, in order to receive notifications of events that are occurring. A producer can then push these notification events to a consumer as they arrive. Alternatively, if a consumer is slow, it can pull notification events according to its own consumption rate. The end-to-end system of a producer and its consumers is known as a **pipeline**. It is important to note that pipelines are lazy by default and do not materialize until they are subscribed to by a consumer. This is very different from eager Java types, like Future, which represent active work. The ReactiveX API consists of the following components:

1. **Observables**: Observables represent the core concept of ReactiveX. They represent the sequences of emitted items, and they generate events that are propagated to the intended subscribers.

2. **Observer:** Any application can express its intent for events published by an observable by creating an observer and subscribing to the respective observable. The intent is expressed in terms of the `OnNext`, `OnCompleted`, and `OnError` methods. Each observable sends a stream of events, followed by a completion event, which executes these methods.

3. **Operators**: Operators enable us to transform, combine, and manipulate the sequences of items emitted by observables. The operators on an observable provide a new observable, and thus, they can be tied together. They do not work independently on the original observable; instead, they work on the observable generated by the previous operator to generate a new observable. The complete operator chain is lazy. It is not evaluated until an observer is subscribed to it. The complete chain is shown as follows:

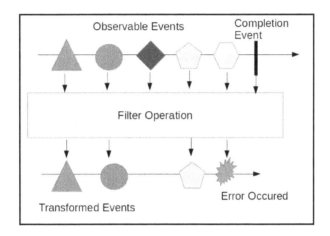

ReactiveX provides the architecture design to build reactive applications. Individual libraries were built around it in different imperative languages to enable its use. These abstractions allow us to build asynchronous, non-blocking applications, and provide the additional benefits listed in the following sections.

Composite streams

In software design, **composition** refers to grouping different entities and treating each group as a single entity. Additionally, the single entity exhibits the same behavior as the type it refers to. ReactiveX streams are composite in nature. They make it possible to combine existing data streams, add transformations, and generate new data streams. Moreover, all of this can be done in a declarative manner, making the overall solution maintainable in the long run.

Flexible operators

The libraries offer a range of operators for all kinds of functions. Each of the operators accomplishes its tasks similarly to that of a workstation on an assembly line. It takes input from the previous workstation and provides input to the next workstation. These operators offer all kinds of data transformation, stream orchestration, and error handlers.

ReactiveX makes its easier to build event-based applications. However, the framework does not present the ways in which different event-driven applications should interact with each other. In a microservice architecture consisting of numerous event-driven services, the gains made are often offset by the workarounds required for inter-process communication.

Reactive Streams

Reactive Streams is a specification that determines the minimum set of interfaces required to build the asynchronous processing of a large volume of unbounded data. It is a specification aimed at JVM and JavaScript runtime. The main goal of the Reactive Streams specification is to standardize the exchange of stream data across an asynchronous boundary of applications. The API consists of the following four interfaces:

1. **Publisher**: The publisher is responsible for the generation of an unbounded number of asynchronous events and pushing those events to the associated subscribers.

2. **Subscriber**: The subscriber is a consumer of the events published by a publisher. The subscriber gets events for subscription, data, completion, and error. It can choose to perform actions on any of them.

3. **Subscription**: A subscription is a shared context between the publisher and subscriber, for the purpose of mediating the data exchange between the two. The subscription is available with the subscriber only, and enables it to control the flow of events from the publisher. The subscription becomes invalid if there is an error or a completion. A subscriber can also cancel the subscriptions, in order to close its stream.

4. **Processor**: The processor represents a stage of data processing between a subscriber and a publisher. Consequently, it is bound by both of them. The processor has to obey the contract between the publisher and the subscriber. If there is an error, it must propagate it back to the subscriber.

The Reactive Streams specification is the result of a collaborative effort of engineers from Kaazing, Netflix, Pivotal, Red Hat, Twitter, Typesafe, and many other companies.

While there are only four interfaces, there are around 30 rules that govern the data exchange between the publisher and the subscriber. These rules are based on the two principles covered in the following sections.

Asynchronous processing

Asynchronous execution refers to the ability to execute tasks without having to wait to finish previously executed tasks first. The execution model decouples tasks, so that each of them can be performed simultaneously, utilizing the available hardware.

The Reactive Streams API delivers events in an asynchronous manner. A publisher can generate event data in a synchronous blocking manner. On the other hand, each of the on-event handlers can process the events in a synchronously blocking manner. However, event publishing must occur asynchronously. It must not be blocked by the subscriber while processing events.

Subscriber backpressure

A subscriber can control events in its queue to avoid any overruns. It can also request more events if there is additional capacity. Backpressure enforces the publisher to bound the event queues according to the subscriber. Furthermore, a subscriber can ask to receive one element at a time, building a stop-and-wait protocol. It can also ask for multiple elements. On the other hand, a publisher can apply the appropriate buffers to hold non-delivered events, or it can just start to drop events if the production rate is more than the consumption rate.

It is important to note that the Reactive Streams API is aimed at the flow of events between different systems. Unlike ReactiveX, it does not provide any operators to perform transformations. The API has been adopted as a part of the `java.util.concurrent.Flow` package in JDK 9.

David Karnok's classification

David Karnok, a veteran of various reactive projects like Rxjava and Reactor, has categorized the evolution of reactive libraries into the following generations.

Zero generation

The zero generation revolves around the `java.util.observable` interface and the related callbacks. It essentially uses the observable design pattern for reactive development. It lacks the necessary support of composition, operators, and backpressure.

First generation

The first generation represents Erik Mejer's attempt to address reactive issues by building Rx.NET. This referred to implementations in the form of the `IObserver` and `IObservable` interfaces. The overall design was synchronous and lacked backpressure.

Second generation

The first generation deficiencies of backpressure and synchronous handling were handled in the second generation APIs. This generation refers to the first implementations of Reactive Extensions, such as RxJava 1.X and Akka.

Third generation

The third generation refers to the Reactive Streams specification, which enables library implementors to be compatible with each other and compose sequences, cancellations, and backpressure across boundaries. It also enables an end user to switch between implementations at their own will.

Fourth generation

The fourth generation refers to the fact that reactive operators can be combined in an external or internal fashion, leading to performance optimization. A fourth generation reactive API looks like a third generation, but internally, the operators have changed significantly to yield intended benefits. Reactor 3.0 and RxJava 2.x belong to this generation.

Fifth generation

The fifth generation refers to a future work, in which there will be a need for bidirectional reactive I/O operations over the streams.

Reactor

Reactor is an implementation completed by the Pivotal Open Source team, conforming to the Reactive Streams API. The framework enables us to build reactive applications, taking care of backpressure and request handling. The library offers the following features.

Infinite data streams

Reactor offers implementations for generating infinite sequences of data. At the same time, it offers an API for publishing a single data entry. This is suited to the request-response model. Each API offers methods aimed at handling the specific data cardinality.

Rather than waiting for the entire data collection to arrive, subscribers to each data stream can process items as they arrive. This yields optimized data processing, in terms of space and time. The memory requirement is limited to a subset of items arriving at the same time, rather than the entire collection. In terms of time, results start to arrive as soon as the first element is received, rather than waiting for the entire dataset.

Push-pull model

Reactor is a push-pull system. A fast producer raises events and waits for the slower subscriber to pull them. In the case of a slow publisher and a fast subscriber, the subscriber waits for events to be pushed from the producer. The Reactive Streams API allows this data flow to be dynamic in nature. It only depends on the real-time rate of production and the rate of consumption.

Concurrency agnostic

The Reactor execution model is a concurrency agnostic. It does not cover how different streams should be processed. The library facilitates different execution models, which can be used at a developer's discretion. All transformations are thread safe. There are various operators that can influence the execution model by combining different synchronous streams.

Operator vocabulary

Reactor provides a wide range of operators. These operators allow us to select, filter, transform, and combine streams. The operations are performed as a workstation in a pipeline. They can be combined with each other to build high-level, easy-to-reason data pipelines.

Reactor has been adopted in Spring Framework 5.0 to provide reactive features. The complete project consists of the following sub-projects:

- **Reactor-Core**: This project provides the implementation for the Reactive Streams API. The project is also the foundation for Spring Framework 5.0 Reactive Extensions.
- **Reactor-Extra**: This project complements the Reactor-Core project. It provides the necessary operators to work on top of the Reactive Streams API.
- **Reactor-Tests**: This project contains utilities for test verification.
- **Reactor-IPC**: This project provides non-blocking, inter-process communication. It also provides backpressure-ready network engines for HTTP (including WebSockets), TCP, and UDP. The module can also be used to build microservices.

Project setup

This book follows a hands-on approach; you will learn Reactor by working with examples. This chapter will set up the project that we will use throughout this book. Before we can move on, we will have to do some setting up. Please install the following items on your machine:

- **Java 8**: Reactor works with Java 8 or above. Please download the latest update of Java 8 from the official Oracle website at http://www.oracle.com/technetwork/java/javase/downloads/index.html. At the time of writing, the Java version was 1.8.0_101. You can check your Java version by running the following command:

```
$ java -version
java version "1.8.0_101"
Java(TM) SE Runtime Environment (build 1.8.0_101-b13)
Java HotSpot(TM) 64-Bit Server VM (build 25.101-b13, mixed mode)
```

- **IntelliJ IDEA 2018.1 or above**: We will be using the latest community edition of IntelliJ. You can download the latest version from the JetBrains website at `https://www.jetbrains.com/idea/download/`. We will be using version 2018.1.1.

- **Gradle**: Gradle is a one of the most popular build tools in the JVM ecosystem. It is used for dependency management and for running automated tasks. You don't have to install Gradle on your local machine; we will use a Gradle wrapper that downloads and installs Gradle for your project. To learn more about Gradle, you can refer to the Gradle documentation at `https://docs.gradle.org/current/userguide/userguide.html`.

Now that we have all the prerequisites, let's create a Gradle project by using IntelliJ IDEA itself:

1. Launch IntelliJ IDEA and you will see the following screen, where you can begin to create a project:

2. Click on **Create New Project** to start the process of creating a Java Gradle project. You will see a screen for creating a new project. Here, select **Gradle** and **Java**, as shown in the following screenshot. You will also have to specify the **Project SDK**. Click on the **New** button to select **JDK 8**. Then, click on **Next** to move to the next screen:

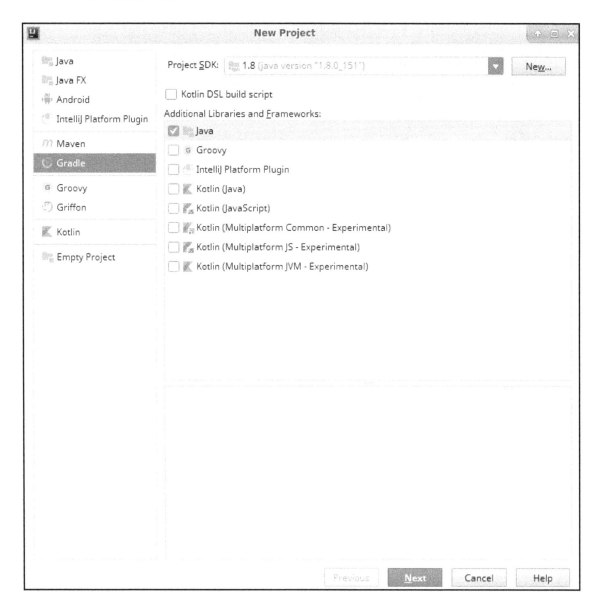

3. Now you will be asked to enter the **GroupId** and **ArtifactId**. Click on **Next** to move to the next screen:

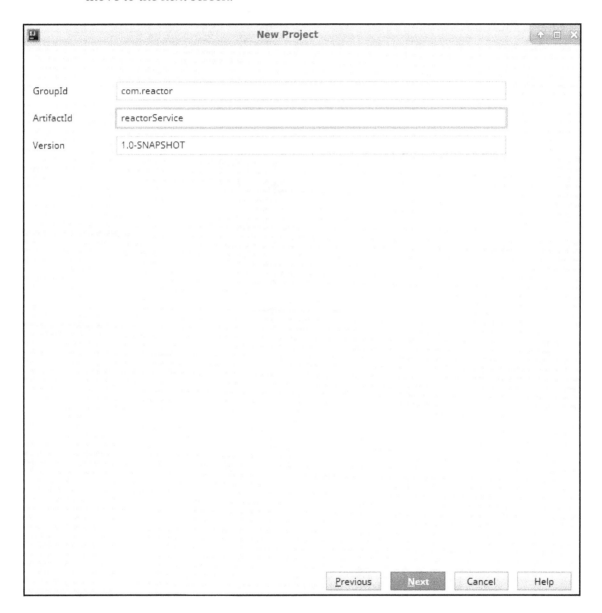

4. The next screen will ask you to specify a few Gradle settings. We will select **Use auto-import**, so that Gradle will automatically add new dependencies when we add them to the build file. Click on **Next** to move to the final screen:

5. On this screen, you will be asked for the location where you want to create the project. Select a convenient directory path for the application. Finally, click on **Finish** to complete the project creation process:

Now that the Java Gradle project has been created, we have to make a couple of changes in the Gradle build file, that is, `build.gradle`. Open the `build.gradle` file in IDE and change it to match the following contents:

```
plugins {
    id "io.spring.dependency-management" version "1.0.5.RELEASE"
}
group 'com.reactor'
version '1.0-SNAPSHOT'
apply plugin: 'java'
sourceCompatibility = 1.8
repositories {
    mavenCentral()
}
dependencyManagement {
    imports {
        mavenBom "io.projectreactor:reactor-bom:Bismuth-RELEASE"
    }
}
dependencies {
    compile 'io.projectreactor:reactor-core'
    testCompile group: 'junit', name: 'junit', version: '4.12'
}
```

In the preceding `build.gradle` file, we have done the following:

1. Added the `io.spring.dependency-management` plugin. This plugin allows us to have a `dependency-management` section, for configuring dependency versions.
2. Configured the `dependency-management` plugin to download the latest version of Reactor. We have used the maven BOM published by the Reactor project.
3. Added the `reactor-core` dependency to the list of project dependencies.

That's all we need to do to start using Reactor.

 At the time of writing, Bismuth-RELEASE was the latest version of Reactor.

Now, let's build a simple test case to see how we can work with the Reactor API. We will build a simple test case for generating Fibonacci numbers. Wikipedia defines Fibonacci numbers as follows:

"In mathematics, the Fibonacci numbers are the numbers in the following integer sequence, called the Fibonacci sequence, and characterized by the fact that every number after the first two is the sum of the two preceding ones:

0 , 1 , 1 , 2 , 3 , 5 , 8 , 13 , 21 , 34 , 55 , 89 , 144, ..."

Let's build our test for the Fibonacci generation. The test case will start to generate a series, from 0 and 1. It will generate the first 50 Fibonacci numbers, and will validate the 50th number as `7778742049`:

```
@Test
public void testFibonacci() {
  Flux<Long> fibonacciGenerator = Flux.generate(
    () -> Tuples.<Long, Long>of(0L, 1L),
    (state, sink) -> {
      sink.next(state.getT1());
      return Tuples.of(state.getT2(), state.getT1() + state.getT2());
    });
    List<Long> fibonacciSeries = new LinkedList<>();
    int size = 50;
    fibonacciGenerator.take(size).subscribe(t -> {
      fibonacciSeries.add(t);
    });
    System.out.println(fibonacciSeries);
    assertEquals( 7778742049L, fibonacciSeries.get(size-1).longValue());
}
```

 The complete code can be found at `https://github.com/ PacktPublishing/Hands-On-Reactive-Programming-with-Reactor/tree/ master/Chapter01`.

In the preceding test case, we are doing the following:

1. We create Fibonacci as `Flux<Long>`, by using the `Flux.generate()` call. The API has a `State` and `Sink`. For now, we will leave the Flux API details for the next chapter.
2. The API takes a seed as `Tuple [0 , 1]`. It then emits the first argument of the pair by using the `Sink.next()` call.

3. The API also generates the next Fibonacci number by aggregating the pair.
4. Next, we select the first 50 Fibonacci numbers by using the `take()` operator.
5. We subscribe to the published numbers, and then append the received number to a `List<Long>`.
6. Finally, we assert the published numbers.

In the preceding test case, we have used a number of Rector features. We will cover each of them in detail in our subsequent chapters. For now, let's execute the test case and check that our project is running fine.

Running our unit test should give us a green bar, as follows:

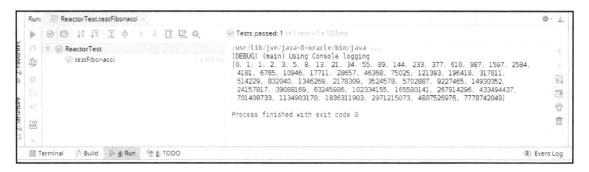

Summary

In this chapter, we discussed the need for a reactive paradigm. We also looked at the evolution of the paradigm, from reactive programming to Reactive Extensions and then Reactive Streams. Furthermore, we discussed the Reactive Streams specification as a specification aimed at JVM for the following:

- Processing a potentially unbounded number of elements in a sequence
- Asynchronously passing elements between components with mandatory non-blocking backpressure

At the end of the chapter, we covered Reactor, an implementation by the Pivotal team, and built a sample project with it. In the next chapter, we will discuss the APIs available in Reactor.

Questions

1. What are the principles of the Reactive Manifesto?
2. What are Reactive Extensions?
3. What does the Reactive Stream specification cater for?
4. What are the principles upon which Reactive Streams are based?
5. What are the salient features of the Reactor Framework?

Further reading

- To learn more about microservice design, please refer to `https://www.packtpub.com/application-development/reactive-microservice-design-video`.
- The Reactive Streams specification is part of Java 9. To find out more about what is included in the Java Development Kit 9, please refer to `https://www.packtpub.com/application-development/reactive-programming-java-9`.

The Publisher and Subscriber APIs in a Reactor

The previous chapter provided you with a brief introduction to the evolution of the reactive paradigm. In that chapter, we discussed how Reactive Streams enable us to perform reactive modeling in imperative languages, such as Java. We also discussed the key components in reactive—the publisher and subscriber. In this chapter, we will cover these two components in detail. Since Reactive Streams is a specification, it does not provide any implementations of the two components. It only lists the responsibilities of the individual components. It is left to implementation libraries, such as Reactor, to provide concrete implementations for the interfaces. Reactor also provides different methods for instantiating publisher and subscriber objects.

We will cover the following topics in this chapter:

- Comparing streams to existing Java APIs
- Understanding the Flux API
- Understanding the Mono API
- Building subscribers to Flux and Mono publishers

Technical requirements

- Java Standard Edition, JDK 8 or above
- IntelliJ IDEA IDE, 2018.1 or above

The GitHub link for this chapter is `https://github.com/PacktPublishing/Hands-On-Reactive-Programming-with-Reactor/tree/master/Chapter02`.

Stream publisher

As we discussed in the previous chapter, the publisher is responsible for the generation of unbounded asynchronous events, and it pushes them to the associated subscribers. It is represented by the `org.reactivestreams.Publisher` interface, as follows:

```
public interface Publisher<T> {
    public void subscribe(Subscriber<? super T> s);
}
```

The interface provides a single `subscribe` method. The method is invoked by any party that is interested in listening to events published by the publisher. The interface is quite simple, and it can be used to publish any type of event, be it a UI event (like a mouse-click) or a data event.

Since the interface is simple, let's add an implementation for our custom `FibonacciPublisher`:

```
public class FibonacciPublisher implements Publisher<Integer> {
    @Override
    public void subscribe(Subscriber<? super Integer> subscriber) {
        int count = 0, a = 0, b = 1;
        while (count < 50) {
            int sum = a + b;
            subscriber.onNext(b);
            a = b;
            b = sum;
            count++;
        }
        subscriber.onComplete();
    }
}
```

This implementation may look good, but does it comply to publisher behavior according to the specification? The specification prescribes rules that describe publisher behavior. A publisher must generate the following four types of events:

- Subscription event
- Data of type T, as declared by the publisher
- Completion event
- Error event

According to the specification, a publisher can emit any number of data events. However, it must publish only one event for completion, error, and subscription. Once a completion or an error event is published, the publisher can no longer send data events back to a subscriber.

As backpressure is an important aspect of the specification, a publisher cannot push an arbitrary number of events to a subscriber. Instead, the subscriber must specify how many events it can receive, and a publisher must publish events equal to, or less than, the specified number.

In order to validate a publisher, the Reactive Streams API has published a test compatibility kit. Let's add the `reactive-streams-tck` in the `build.gradle` to our project:

```
dependencies {
  // rest removed for brevity
  testCompile group: 'org.reactivestreams',
  name: 'reactive-streams-tck', version: '1.0.2'
}
```

The **Technology Compatibility Kit** (**TCK**) provides a `PublisherVerifier` interface that must be implemented in order to validate a publisher. It provides the following two methods:

- `createPublisher(long)`: This method must provide an instance of the publisher that can produce the specified number of events
- `createFailedPublisher()`: This method must try to build a publisher that has raised an error event

Let's add the following implementation to test our `FibonacciPublisher`:

```
public class FibonacciPublisherVerifier extends
PublisherVerification<Integer> {
    public FibonacciPublisherVerifier(){
        super(new TestEnvironment());
    }
    @Override
    public Publisher<Integer> createFailedPublisher() {
        return null;
    }
    @Override
    public Publisher<Integer> createPublisher(long elements) {
        return new FibonacciPublisher();
    }
}
```

Now, let's run the test case to determine whether we comply with the Reactive Streams publisher specification:

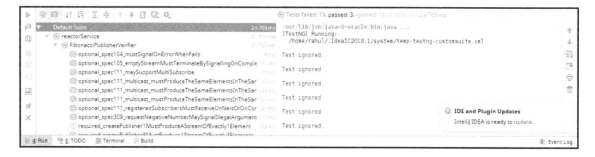

As shown in the preceding screenshot, there are around 20 test failures and 16 skipped tests. We could fix each one of them, but the aim here is to understand that even a simple interface of a publisher is governed by many behavior specifications. Therefore, it is overkill to build a custom publisher. As service builders, we can use the Reactor framework. This provides publisher implementations capable of publishing any kind of data.

Stream subscriber

A subscriber is used to listen to events generated by a publisher. When a subscriber registers to a publisher, it receives events in the following order:

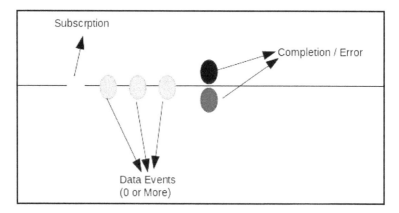

As a result, the subscriber has the following interface to handle all of these events:

```
public interface Subscriber<T> {
    public void onSubscribe(Subscription s);
    public void onNext(T t);
    public void onError(Throwable t);
    public void onComplete();
}
```

Let's cover each of these methods in detail, as follows:

- `onSubscribe(Subscription s)`: As soon as a publisher has received a subscriber, it generates a subscription event. The generated subscription event is then received in the specified method.
- `onNext (T)`: All data events generated by a publisher are received by the subscriber in the specified method. A publisher may or may not publish a data event before closing the stream.
- `onCompletion()`: This refers to the completion event, which must be handled by a subscriber. Once a completion event is received, the subscription is considered void.
- `onError()`: This refers to the error event, which must be handled by a subscriber. An error can occur at any moment—while building a subscription or while generating the next data event. In any case, the publisher must send the error event. Once the event is received, the subscription is considered void.

Subscription

The subscription is an important component in Reactive Streams. It provides the necessary control flow, so that publishers do not over-run a subscriber. This is known as backpressure.

Once the subscriber receives the subscription event, it must request that the publisher publish a specified count of events over their respective subscription. This is done by invoking the `request(long)` method of the subscription object.

As data events are generated, they are received by the subscriber. Once the limit has been reached, the publisher must stop publishing more events. As the subscriber processes these events, it must request additional events from the publisher:

```
public interface Subscription {
    public void request(long n);
    public void cancel();
}
```

The subscription object allows a subscriber to control the events it wants to receive. Whenever the subscriber determines that it no longer wants the events, it can invoke the `cancel()` method of the subscription. Once invoked, a subscriber may receive fewer data events, in accordance with the demand raised before the cancellation. Post-cancellation, the subscription will become void, meaning that it cannot be used to request additional data.

 A value of `Long.MaxValue` for the request method would result in an infinite flow of events from the publisher.

A subscriber can cancel an active subscription with the `onSubscribe()` method before any demand can be raised using the request method. In this case, the publisher will drop the subscription without raising any events.

Now that we have gone over the subscriber interface in detail, we can try to build a `FibonacciSubscriber`, as follows:

```
public class FibonacciSubscriber implements Subscriber<Long> {
    private Subscription sub;
    @Override
    public void onSubscribe(Subscription s) {
        sub = s;
        sub.request(10);
    }
    @Override
    public void onNext(Long fibNumber) {
        System.out.println(fibNumber);
        sub.cancel();
    }
    @Override
    public void onError(Throwable t) {
        t.printStackTrace();
        sub=null;
    }
    @Override
    public void onComplete() {
```

```
        System.out.println("Finished");
        sub=null;
    }
}
```

The preceding implementation does the following things:

1. Upon receiving the subscription event, a request is raised to handle 10 events.
2. When received, all data events are printed to the output console.
3. After processing a single event, the subscriber cancels the subscription.
4. The `onCompletion` method sets the subscription to `null`.
5. The `onError` method prints the error message to the console and sets the subscription as `null`.

Now, let's validate the subscriber by using the `SubscriberBlackboxVerification<T>` abstract class. We need to implement the `createSubsciber()` method, as shown in the following code:

```java
public class FibonacciSubsciberVerification extends
SubscriberBlackboxVerification<Long> {
    public FibonacciSubsciberVerification(){
        super(new TestEnvironment());
    }
    @Override
    public Subscriber<Long> createSubscriber() {
        return new FibonacciSubscriber();
    }
    @Override
    public Long createElement(int element) {
        return new Long(element);
    }
}
```

Let's run the test case to determine whether our subscriber meets the Reactive Streams criteria:

Here, we can also find a large number of broken test cases. These broken test cases define the behavior for a subscriber. We could fix these, but the better option would be to use Reactor to create our services. In the following section, we will describe the publisher and subscriber implementations available in Reactor. These implementations conform to the specification behaviors.

Reactive Streams comparison

Before we jump into Reactor, let's compare the Streams model with some of the existing similar APIs, such as the `java.util.Observable` interface and the JMS API. We will try to determine the similarities and the key differences between the APIs.

The Observable interface

The `java.util.Observable` interface implements the Observer pattern, which can be co-related here. However, all similarities end here. If we look at the `Observable` interface, we have the following methods:

```
public class Observable {
  void addObserver (Observer o);
  void deleteObserver (Observer o);
  void deleteObservers();
  void notifyObservers();
  void notifyObserver(int arg);
  int countObservers();
  boolean hasChanged();
}
```

Let's look at the `Observer` interface before we determine the differences:

```
public interface Observer{
  void update(Observable o, Object arg)
}
```

If we look at the `Observable` and `Observer` interfaces, we can see that they are all about a single event and its state. The Observable API has the responsibility of determining a change and publishing it to all interested parties. On the other hand, the `Observer` only listens to the change. This is not what we are modeling with the `Publisher` and `Subscriber` interface. The `Publisher` interface is responsible for generating unbounded events, unlike the Observable, which is all about single entity state changes. The `Subscriber`, on the other hand, lists all kinds of events, such as data, error, and completion.

Furthermore, the `Observable` maintains an active list of observers. It has the responsibility of removing observers that are no longer interested in the event. This is not the same as the `Publisher`, which is only responsible for subscriptions. The `Subscriber` makes the decision to close the subscription, at its will.

Java Messaging Service API

Let's look at how Reactive Streams compares to the **Java Messaging Service (JMS)** API. The JMS specification describes a `Queue` and a `Topic`, to which a producer and a consumer can connect:

```
@Resource(lookup = "jms/Queue")
private static Queue queue;

@Resource(lookup = "jms/Topic")
private static Topic topic;
Session session = connection.createSession(false,Session.AUTO_ACKNOWLEDGE);
MessageProducer producer = session.createProducer(queue);
MessageConsumer consumer = session.createConsumer(topic)
```

Here, the producer is responsible for generating unbounded events on the queue or topics, while the consumer actively consumes the events. The producer and consumer are working in isolation, at their own rates. The task of managing the subscription is taken care of by the JMS broker. This is different from the Subscription API, where backpressure plays a major role in event generation. There is also no event modeling, like subscription, error, or completion. The JMS connection is like a never-ending stream of data. It cannot provide completion or error events. If we need to support this, custom objects must be modeled first.

Learning about the Reactor Core API

The Reactor project is divided into different modules. The `reactor-core` module is the central library, aimed at providing implementations for Reactive Streams. The library provides Flux and Mono, which are two different implementations of the `Publisher` interface. The two publishers are different in terms of the number of events that they can emit. Flux can emit infinite sequences of elements, but the Mono API makes it possible to emit a maximum of one element. Let's cover these APIs in detail, in the following sections.

The Flux API

`Flux<T>` is a general purpose reactive publisher. It represents a stream of asynchronous events with zero or more values, optionally terminated by either a completion signal or an error. It is important to note that a Flux emits the following three events:

- **Value** refers to the values generated by the publisher
- **Completion** refers to a normal termination of the stream
- **Error** refers to an erroneous termination of the stream:

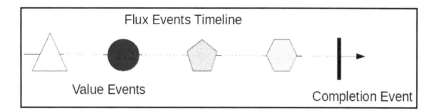

All of the preceding events are optional. This can lead to streams of the following types:

- **Infinite stream**: A publisher generating only value events, and no terminal events (completion and error)
- **Infinite empty stream**: A stream generating no value events and no terminating events
- **Finite stream**: A publisher generating *N* finite values, followed by a terminal event
- **Empty stream**: A publisher generating no value events, and only terminal events

Flux supports the generation of all preceding variations, so it can be used for most of the generic use cases. It can also generate sequences of alerts for an application. The alerts are an infinite stream of values, with no terminal. Flux can also be used to stream order data from an order database. The order values get terminated at the last order value. It may be the case that there are no orders for a particular product type, making the stream empty for that type.

Generating the Flux API

The `Flux<T>` API supports stream generation from various sources, such as individual values, collections, Java 8 streams, and more. It can also be used to generate a stream from a custom logic, or from an existing reactive publisher. We will discuss all of these options in detail in upcoming sections.

The Flux.just method

This is the simplest method for Flux generation. It takes a set of values, such as `var-args`, and generates a finite Flux stream with them. Each of the values specified as `var-args` forms a value event of the Flux. A completion event is published after publishing all of the specified values:

```
Flux.just("Red");
Flux.just("Red", "Blue", "Yellow", "Black");
Flux.just(new Person("Rahul"), new Person("Rudra"));
```

The Flux.from methods

The `From` methods can be used to generate a Flux from various sources, such as arrays, collections, and so on. In this case, all of the values are identified as multi-valued datasets beforehand. The generated Flux publishes the value events for each value in the original dataset, followed by a completion event. The offered methods have the following variants:

- `Flux.fromArray`: This is used to build a stream from an array of a type.
- `Flux.fromIterable`: This is used to build a stream from collections. All collections are of the `Iterable<T>` type, which can be passed to this to generate the intended stream.

- `Flux.fromStream`: This is used to build a Flux from an existing Java 8 stream or a Java 8 stream supplier. Consider the following code:

```
Flux.fromArray(new Integer[]{1,1,2,3,5,8,13});
Flux.fromIterable(Arrays.asList("Red", "Blue", "Yellow", "Black"));
Flux.fromStream(IntStream.range(1,100).boxed());
```

Utility methods

Flux offers methods to generate infinite streams and empty streams, or to convert an existing Reactive Stream publisher to Flux. These methods are required to generate streams that can be combined with other streams, using the available operators, as follows:

- `Flux.empty`: This method generates an empty stream with no values and only completion.
- `Flux.error`: This method generates an error stream with no values and only specified errors.
- `Flux.never`: This method generates a stream with no events at all. It does not generate events of any type.
- `Flux.from`: This method takes an existing reactive publisher and generates a Flux from it.
- `Flux.defer`: This method is used to build a lazy reactive publisher. The method takes a Java 8 supplier to instantiate a subscription-specific Reactive Stream publisher. The publisher instance is only generated when a subscriber makes a subscription to the Flux.

The Flux.generate method

Flux supports programmatic event generation. In the previous chapter, we used the API to generate Fibonacci events. This is an advanced usage method of the API, and it involves some more components. We will cover these in detail in the following sections.

SynchronousSink

The sink gets bounded to a subscriber of the publisher. It gets invoked via the consumer function, when a subscriber asks for data. For each invocation, the sink can be used to generate a maximum of one value event at a time. The sink can raise additional `onCompletion` or error events during the invocation.

It is important to note that the events generated by sink are synchronously consumed at the subscriber end. Let's reflect on the Fibonacci test that we wrote in the previous chapter:

```
Flux<Long> fibonacciGenerator = Flux.generate(
        () -> Tuples.<Long, Long>of(0L, 1L),
        (state, sink) -> {
            sink.next(state.getT1());
            System.out.println("generated "+state.getT1());
            return Tuples.of(state.getT2(), state.getT1() +
state.getT2());
        });
fibonacciGenerator.take(size).subscribe(t -> {
    System.out.println("consuming "+t);
    fibonacciSeries.add(t);
});
```

Generating more that one event in the sink leads to `java.lang.IllegalStateException: More than one call to onNext.`

We have added additional print statements while generating and consuming numbers. Let's run our tests to see the output, as follows:

The consumer and producer statements are generated in an alternative manner. We can easily deduce that each number is consumed before the next number is generated. The Generate API is offered in multiple variants, and the sink can be used with or without an initial state. In our `FibonacciGenerator`, we used this with a state that is initialized on a per-subscriber basis. Optionally, we can also provide a terminal function, which gets invoked upon the termination of the events stream. This means that it will occur after the sink invokes an error or completion event. The terminal function can be used to perform any cleanup associated with the state.

Flux.create

`Flux.create` is another mechanism for generating events programmatically. It takes a `FluxSink`, which is capable of generating any number of events. The API is more generic than the `Generate` methods discussed in the previous section. The `FluxSink` is capable of generating events asynchronously. Moreover, it does not take subscription cancellation or backpressure into account. This means that even if the subscriber has cancelled its subscription, the create API will continue to generate events. All implementations must listen for the `cancel` event and explicitly initiate stream closure.

As for backpressure, the producer keeps generating the events without looking into any demand from the subscriber. These events are buffered and dropped by default if the subscription is lost.

To see how the two are different, let's modify our `FibonacciGenerator` to use a `FluxSink`. Some of the key differences are highlighted as follows:

- There is no initial seed state in the API
- The `FluxSink` keeps generating the events, irrespective of the subscription state
- We can generate any number of events in the sink
- The `OnDispose` event can be listened to in order to perform any cleanup, or to stop publishing events
- All events that are generated are buffered and dropped once the subscription is cancelled

It is important to note that the `FluxSink` provides lifecycle callback methods, which can be used to perform additional cleanups, or any other action, as follows:

- `OnCancel`: This method gets invoked when the subscription is cancelled.
- `OnDispose`: This method gets invoked when the subscription is closed due to a cancel, close, or error event.
- `OnRequest`: This method is invoked with the value specified by the subscriber. It can be used to build a pull data model. When the method is invoked, the next method can be invoked for the specified number of the values:

```
@Test
public void testFibonacciFluxSink() {
    Flux<Long> fibonacciGenerator = Flux.create(e -> {
        long current = 1, prev = 0;
        AtomicBoolean stop = new AtomicBoolean(false);
        e.onDispose(()->{
            stop.set(true);
```

```
            System.out.println("******* Stop Received ****** ");
        });
        while (current > 0) {
            e.next(current);
            System.out.println("generated " + current);
            long next = current + prev;
            prev = current;
            current = next;
        }
        e.complete();
    });
    List<Long> fibonacciSeries = new LinkedList<>();
    fibonacciGenerator.take(50).subscribe(t -> {
        System.out.println("consuming " + t);
        fibonacciSeries.add(t);
    });
    System.out.println(fibonacciSeries);
}
```

Let's check the output that's generated, as follows:

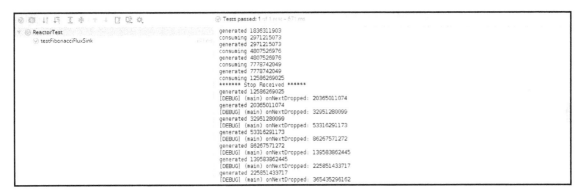

Flux also provides a `Push` method. This is similar to the `create` method,
but the process of how error and complete events are invoked varies.
These events must be invoked in a synchronous manner, from a single
thread producer.

The Mono API

Now that we have covered the Flux API, let's look at Mono. It is capable of generating a maximum of one event. This is a specific use case for Flux, capable of handling one response model, such as data aggregation, HTTP request-response, service invocation response, and so on. It is important to note that a Mono emits the following three events:

- **Value** refers to the single value generated by the publisher
- **Completion** refers to a normal termination of the stream
- **Error** refers to an erroneous termination of the stream

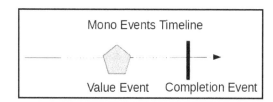

Since Mono is a subset of Flux, it supports a subset of Flux operators. Let's look at how to build a Mono.

Generating a Mono

The Mono<T> API supports stream generation from various single-value sources, like individual values, method invocations, Java 8 supplier functions, and so on. It can also be used to generate a stream from a custom logic or from an existing reactive publisher. We will now discuss these in detail.

The Mono.just method

The Mono.just method is the simplest method for Mono generation. It takes a single value and generates a finite Mono stream from it. A completion event is published after publishing the specified value:

```
Mono.just("Red");
Mono.justOrEmpty(value);
Mono.justOrEmpty(Optional.empty());
```

The Mono.from method

The `From` methods are used to build a Flux when the value can be determined from an existing source. Unlike the Flux methods, where the sources are multi-valued, the sources for Mono are single-valued. These methods are offered in the following variants:

- `fromCallable`: This method generates Mono with one value, followed by the completion event. If multi-valued datasets, like arrays or collections, are returned from `Callable`, then the complete dataset is pushed as an object in the single event.
- `fromFuture`: This method generates Mono with one value, followed by the completion event.
- `fromSupplier`: This method generates Mono with one value, followed by the completion event.
- `fromRunnable`: This method generates Mono with no value and only a completion event. This can be explained by using the following code:

```
Mono.fromSupplier(() -> 1);
Mono.fromCallable(() -> new String[]{"color"}).subscribe(t ->
System.out.println("received " + t));
Mono.fromRunnable(() -> System.out.println(" ")).subscribe(t ->
System.out.println("received " + t), null, () ->
System.out.println("Finished"));
```

Utility methods

Mono offers methods to generate empty/error streams or to convert an existing Reactive Stream publisher to Mono. These methods are required to generate streams that can be combined with others by using the available operators, as follows:

- `Mono.empty`: Generates a stream with no value and only a completion.
- `Mono.error`: Generates a stream with no value and only a specified error.
- `Mono.never`: Generates a stream with no events at all. It does not generate an event of any type.
- `Mono.from`: Generates a Mono stream from an existing stream publisher.
- `Mono.defer`: This method is used to build a lazy reactive publisher. It also takes a Java 8 supplier to instantiate a subscription-specific Reactive Stream publisher. The publisher instance is only generated when a subscriber makes a subscription to the Mono.

It is important to note that a Mono can be generated by using a Flux source. In that case, Mono uses the first event published from the Flux, as follows:

```
Mono.from(Flux.just("Red", "Blue", "Yellow", "Black")).subscribe(t ->
System.out.println("received " + t))

**** Output ******
received Red

Process finished with exit code 0
```

Mono.create

In addition to the `Flux.create` methods, there is a `Mono.create` method. This method provides a `MonoSink`, which can be used to generate a value, completion, or error event. Unlike the Flux methods, where we are generating *N* events, if we generate more events in Mono, they are dropped. There is also no handling for backpressure, as there is only one event.

The API does not take subscription cancellations into account. This means that even if the subscriber has cancelled its subscription, the create method still generates its event. Implementors must register custom hooks to lifecycle events and perform stream closures.

Building subscribers to Flux and Mono

Reactor Flux and Mono provide a wide choice of subscribe methods. Reactive publishers raise four types of events, namely subscription, value, completion, and error. Individual functions can be registered for each of the events. We can also register a subscriber without listening to any kind of event. Let's look at all of the possible variants offered, as follows:

```
fibonacciGenerator.subscribe(); (1)

fibonacciGenerator.subscribe(t -> System.out.println("consuming " + t));
(2)

fibonacciGenerator.subscribe(t -> System.out.println("consuming " + t),
                e -> e.printStackTrace() ); (3)

fibonacciGenerator.subscribe(t -> System.out.println("consuming " + t),
                e -> e.printStackTrace(),
                ()-> System.out.println("Finished")); (4)

fibonacciGenerator.subscribe(t -> System.out.println("consuming " + t),
```

```
        e -> e.printStackTrace(),
        ()-> System.out.println("Finished"),
        s -> System.out.println("Subscribed :"+ s)); (5)
```

The preceding code shows all of the `Subscribe` methods:

1. No event is consumed, as shown in line 1.
2. Only value events are consumed, as shown in line 2.
3. Along with value events, we also print error stack-trace, as shown in line 3.
4. We can listen to value, error, and completion events, as shown in line 4.
5. We can listen to value, error, completion, and subscription events, as shown in line 5.

> All `Subscribe` methods return a `Disposable` type. This type can also be used to cancel the subscription.

At times, we may determine that the `Subscribe` methods are not good enough. We must create a custom subscriber with its own handling. Reactor provides a `reactor.core.publisher.BaseSubsciber<T>` for these situations. Instead of implementing the Reactive Stream `Subscriber`, reactor recommends implementing the `BaseSubscriber` abstract class:

```
BaseSubscriber<Long> fibonacciSubsciber= new BaseSubscriber<Long>() {
        @Override
        protected void hookOnSubscribe(Subscription subscription) { }

        @Override
        protected void hookOnNext(Long value) {}

        @Override
        protected void hookOnComplete() { }

        @Override
        protected void hookOnError(Throwable throwable) {}

        @Override
        protected void hookOnCancel() {}
    };
```

If we look at the `BaseSubscriber` implementation, we will see the following:

- Each individual event can be handled in a separate hook method.
- It captures the subscription and makes it accessible by using the upstream method. This method can be invoked in any lifecycle method.
- It also handles backpressure by providing `request(long)` methods. The default method is to request values one by one. However, the subscriber can raise additional demands by using the `request` method.
- It also presents the `requestUnbound()` method, which disables backpressures.

Once we have the custom subscriber, it can be invoked by using the `subscribe()` method, available with Flux and Mono.

Lifecycle hooks

The publisher-subscriber communication generates events throughout the lifecycle of a Reactive Stream. Reactor provides corresponding lifecycle methods that can be used to hook custom logic to each of the said events, as shown in the following table:

Event	Method
Subscribe event	`doOnSubscribe`
Request event, for *N* items from the subscriber	`doOnRequest`
Value event, for all generated values	`doOnNext`
Error event, for any error by the publisher	`doOnError`
Completion event	`doOnCompletion`
Cancel event, for cancellation by the subscriber	`doOnCancel`

In addition to the preceding methods, there are the following methods:

- `doOnEach`: This method is executed for all publisher events raised in the stream processing.
- `doOnTerminate`: This method is executed for stream closure due to an error or completion. It does not take cancellation into account.
- `doFinally`: This method is executed for stream closures due to errors, completions, or cancellations.

Trying a hands-on project

Now that we have discussed Reactor interfaces in detail, let's try to generate a factorial series using Reactor. Given a number, we want to generate a factorial of all numbers less than or equal to the provided number. In number theory, a factorial is described as follows:

> *"The factorial of a positive number 'n' is defined as n! = n(n-1)(n-2)...2.1 For example, 5 ! = 5 × 4 × 3 × 2 × 1 = 120."*

Now, let's try to build a factorial stream function that takes a number and attempts to generate a factorial for every number, from 0 to *N*:

```
public class FactorialService {

    Flux<Double> generateFactorial(long number) {
        Flux<Double> factorialStream = Flux.generate(
                () -> Tuples.<Long, Double>of(0L, 1.0d),
                (state, sink) -> {
                    Long factNumber = state.getT1();
                    Double factValue = state.getT2();
                    if (factNumber <= number)
                        sink.next(factValue);
                    else
                        sink.complete();
                    return Tuples.of(factNumber + 1, (factNumber + 1) *
factValue);
                });
        return factorialStream;
    }
}
```

In the preceding code, we performed the following:

1. The initial `factorialNumber` was set to `0`, with the factorial as `1`.
2. We then checked whether the `factorialNumber` was less than or equal to the passed number, and published the factorial value for it.
3. If `factorialNumber` is more than the passed number, then we publish the completion.
4. We incremented the `factorialNumber` and computed the factorial for it.

The preceding flow is quite simple, but it makes it possible to utilize various Flux components. Since the factorial service is ready, we need to validate it by subscribing to it. In the following test case, we do the following things:

1. Invoke the generator for factorial numbers up to `10`.
2. Display each generated number by using the `doOnNext()` lifecycle hook.
3. Use the `last()` operator to get the last value. We will cover operators in the next chapter.
4. Compare and assert the value in the subscriber value event function:

```java
public class FactorialServiceTest {

    @Test
    public void testFactorial() {
        Flux<Double> factorialGenerator = new
FactorialService().generateFactorial(10);
        factorialGenerator
                .doOnNext(t -> System.out.println(t))
                .last()
                .subscribe(t -> assertEquals(3628800.0, t, 0.0));
    }
}
```

Now, let's run the test case to view the output:

Summary

In this chapter, we provided a detailed discussion of the publisher and the subscriber interfaces of Reactive Streams. We attempted to implement these interfaces to illustrate that there are many non-explicit rules for them. These rules have been converted into the Reactive Streams TCK, against which all implementations should be validated. We also compared the publisher-subscriber pattern with the existing Observer and JMS patterns used in Java. Next, we took a detailed look at the Flux and Mono implementations available in Reactor. We looked at methods for creating them, and then subscribed to the generated streams.

In the next chapter, we will look at the operators that can be used to modify the generated streams.

Questions

1. How can we validate Reactive Stream publisher and subscriber implementations?
2. How is the Reactive Stream publisher-subscriber model different from the JMS API?
3. How is the Reactive Stream publisher-subscriber model different from the Observer API?
4. What is the difference between Flux and Mono?
5. What is the difference between `SynchronousSink` and `FluxSink`?
6. What are the different lifecycle hooks available in Reactor?

Further reading

- For more information, please refer to the video under the Reactive Streams specification, as this is part of Java 9: `https://www.packtpub.com/application-development/reactive-java-9-video`
- To gain in-depth knowledge on building microservices using Akka as a Reactive Streams library, please refer to the following video: `https://www.packtpub.com/application-development/building-microservice-akka-http-video`

Data and Stream Processing 3

In the previous chapter, we generated streams of data by using a Reactor Flux and then consumed it in a subscriber. Reactor also provides a diverse set of operators that can be used to manipulate data. These operators take a stream as input and then generate another stream of another type of data. In a nutshell, these operators provide a powerful way to compose readable data pipelines. There are various operators for filtering, mapping, and collecting data. All of them will be covered in this chapter.

This chapter will cover the following topics:

- Filtering data
- Converting data

Technical requirements

- Java Standard Edition, JDK 8 or above
- IntelliJ IDEA IDE, 2018.1 or above

The GitHub link for this chapter is `https://github.com/PacktPublishing/Hands-On-Reactive-Programming-with-Reactor/tree/master/Chapter03`.

Generating data

Before we jump into working with various operators, let's first generate a stream of data. In order to do this, let's revisit our Fibonacci series from `Chapter 1`, *Getting Started with Reactive Streams*.

In number theory, Fibonacci numbers are characterized by the fact that every number after the first two numbers is the sum of the two preceding ones (that is, 0 , 1 , 1 , 2 , 3 , 5 , 8 , 13 ,21 , 34 , 55 , 89 , 144, and so on).

The Flux generated API enables us to build a generator. These generators start the series from 0 and 1. All numbers are printed to the console by a subscriber, which listens to all of the generated events. This is shown in the following code:

```
Flux<Long> fibonacciGenerator = Flux.generate(() -> Tuples.<Long,
Long>of(0L, 1L),(state, sink) -> {
   if (state.getT1() < 0)
      sink.complete();
   else
      sink.next(state.getT1());
   return Tuples.of(state.getT2(), state.getT1() + state.getT2());
});
fibonacciGenerator.subscribe(t -> {
   System.out.println(t);
});
```

Let's recap what is happening here, as follows:

- We create the Fibonacci series as `Flux<Long>` by using the `Flux.generate()` call. The API has a state and sink.
- The API takes a seed as `Tuple [0 , 1]`. It then emits the first argument of the pair by using the `Sink.next()` call.
- The API also generates the next Fibonacci number, by aggregating the pair.
- The publisher marks the stream as complete when we generate negative numbers. This is due to their being out of range of the long data type.
- We subscribe to the published numbers, then print the received number to the console. This is shown in the following screenshot:

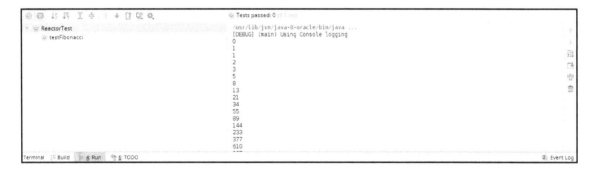

Filtering data

Let's start with the most simple operator for selecting data. There are different analogies of data filtration, as follows:

- Select or reject data based on a given condition
- Select or reject a subset of the generated data

The preceding information is depicted in the following diagram:

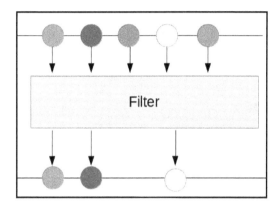

The filter() operator

The `filter()` operator enables selection of the data on the passed condition. The API takes a Boolean predicate, which is evaluated for every emitted value, in order to determine whether it is selected. Filtering is quite common. Let's suppose that we want to select dates based on a month range, or we want to select employee data based on employee IDs. In those cases, the Boolean predicate passed to the filter holds the selection logic. This can be quite flexible, and can be adapted to different needs.

Let's extend our Fibonacci generator to only select even numbers, as follows:

```
fibonacciGenerator.filter(a -> a%2 == 0).subscribe(t -> {
    System.out.println(t);
});
```

In the preceding code, the predicate performs a divisibility check. If the number is divisible by 2, the operator performs a predicate evaluation in a synchronous manner. If the condition is satisfied, the value is passed to the subscriber.

There is also a `FilterWhen`, which is an asynchronous manner of Boolean evaluation. This takes the input value and provides the Boolean publisher in return. This can be explained with the following code:

```
fibonacciGenerator.filterWhen(a -> Mono.just(a < 10)).subscribe(t -> {
    System.out.println(t);
});
```

In the preceding code, the predicate performs a less-than check. This is a deferred evaluation, and the result is returned as a `Mono<Boolean>`.

The take operator

The filter methods discussed previously enable us to select data. If we want to select the top 10 elements, for example, we can use the `filter` operator, with a predicate that has a counter. Alternatively, there is a `take` operator for this purpose. The operator takes a number and selects the specified number of elements, as follows:

```
fibonacciGenerator.take(10).subscribe(t -> {
    System.out.println(t);
});
```

The preceding code will select the first 10 values to form the Fibonacci generator.

Now, let's suppose that we want to select the last 10 elements. The `takeLast` operator is designed for this purpose. It also maintains a count and selects elements from the end of the series:

```
fibonacciGenerator.takeLast(10).subscribe(t -> {
    System.out.println(t);
});
```

 If the stream is truly unbounded, there will not be any last elements. The operator only works when there is a normal close of the stream.

If we only want to select the last value, we can use the `takeLast(1)` operator. This operator will give back a Flux stream containing just one value. Alternatively, there is a `last()` operator, which gives back a Mono publisher that consists of the last published element. The use of the `last` operator is shown as follows:

```
fibonacciGenerator.last().subscribe(t -> {
    System.out.println(t);
});
```

The skip operator

Now that we have found ways to select data, let's look at ways to reject data. The Reactor API offers diverse methods to reject data. There is a skip operator, with the following types:

- `Skip(count)`: This will reject the specified number of elements from the beginning of the stream.
- `Skip(Duration)`: This will reject elements for the said duration from the beginning of the stream.
- `SkipLast(count)`: This will reject a specified number of elements from the end of the stream.
- `SkipUntil(Boolean Predicate)`: This will reject elements until the first occurrence of the said condition is true.

The preceding commands are shown in the following code:

```
fibonacciGenerator.skip(10).subscribe(t -> {
    System.out.println(t);
});
fibonacciGenerator.skip(Duration.ofMillis(10)).subscribe(t -> {
    System.out.println(t);
});
fibonacciGenerator.skipUntil(t -> t > 100).subscribe(t -> {
    System.out.println(t);
});
```

The preceding code sample has the following variants:

- The first subscriber rejects the first `10` elements and prints the rest of them
- The second subscriber prints the elements after rejecting the elements for `10` milliseconds
- The second subscriber prints the elements after the first data element goes beyond `100`

The output is shown in the following screenshot:

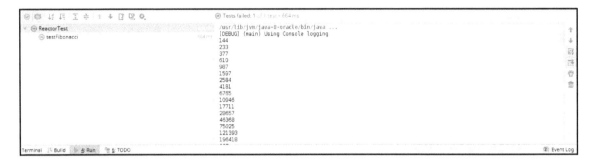

Until now, we have discussed generic ways to select and reject data. However, the Flux interface offers the following special operators for filtering data in specific scenarios:

- `distinct`: This operator is used to select unique elements of the passed data stream
- `distintUntilChanged`: This operator is used to select the first set of distinct items
- `ignoreElements`: This operator is used to completely ignore the data elements
- `single`: This operator is used to select only a single data element
- `elementAt`: This operator selects the element at the specified index of the stream

In the preceding section, we discussed ways to select or reject data. Reactor offers many operators for this purpose. It is often a good idea to check the API and determine whether there is an operator for the intended purpose rather than customize the predicate with the filter and skip methods.

Converting data

It is often necessary to convert data from one format to another. The reactor provides a vast set of operators to achieve this. Not only can we convert data but we can modify the amount of data elements as well.

The map() operator

From the preceding Fibonacci example that was used to explain the `skip()` operator, suppose that we want to convert the first 10 elements into Roman numeral equivalents.

Roman numerals are represented by seven letters: I, V, X, L, C, D, and M. These letters represent 1, 5, 10, 50, 100, 500, and 1,000, respectively. The seven letters can be combined to represent thousands of numbers. The Roman numeral scheme used letters as tally markers. Markers were combined to represent unit values.

We have a long number and we want to convert it to its Roman equivalent; this is where the `map()` operator is valuable. It applies a transformation to each and every value of the existing stream, as follows:

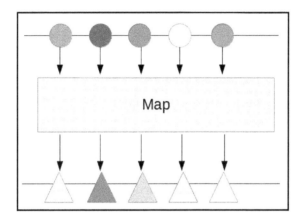

In order to achieve this transformation, we need a `RomanNumberConvertor`. In the following code, we have defined a conversion from integers to their Roman equivalents:

```
class RomanNumber {
    TreeMap<Integer, String> romanMap= new TreeMap<>();
    RomanNumber(){
        romanMap.put(1000, "M");
        romanMap.put(900, "CM");
        romanMap.put(500, "D");
        romanMap.put(400, "CD");
        romanMap.put(100, "C");
        romanMap.put(90, "XC");
        romanMap.put(50, "L");
        romanMap.put(40, "XL");
        romanMap.put(10, "X");
        romanMap.put(9, "IX");
        romanMap.put(5, "V");
        romanMap.put(4, "IV");
        romanMap.put(1, "I");
    }
    String toRomanNumeral(int number) {
        int l =  romanMap.floorKey(number);
        if ( number == l ) {
```

```
                return romanMap.get(number);
        }
        return romanMap.get(1) + toRomanNumeral(number-1);
    }
}
```

Since we know how to convert an integer, we will define the Map function for our stream processor. The operator will take the long Value as an input and will then generate the Roman equivalent as a string:

```
RomanNumber numberConvertor= new RomanNumber();
fibonacciGenerator.skip(1).take(10).map(t->
numberConvertor.toRomanNumeral(t.intValue())).subscribe(t -> {
    System.out.println(t);
});
```

A couple of things are done in the preceding code, as follows:

- The skip(1) operator has been used. In the last section, we mentioned that this will skip the first element of the series. This happens because 0 has no Roman equivalent.
- The take(10) operator has been used. This will select only 10 elements from the generated series. This is done to limit the number to less than 1,000.
- The map() operator defines the conversion of longValue to the Roman-equivalent string.
- All of the preceding operators have been chained together to generate one single stream. The output is shown in the following screenshot:

As you can see in the preceding output, the value transformation from number to Roman numeral is applied to each item flowing through the stream.

The flatMap operator

The preceding transformation example that used the `map()` operator was effective when we had a one-to-one value conversion, but it could not handle a one-to-*n* value conversion. We can show this premise by generating a stream of factors for our Fibonacci numbers. Let's first revise what factorization is.

In number theory, factorization is the breakup of a composite number into a product of smaller numbers. For 6, for example, the factors are 1, 2, 3, and 6.

Let's try to convert Fibonacci numbers to their corresponding factors. Each number of the series must be converted to all possible factors. First, let's build a simple function to compute factors:

```
class Factorization {
    Collection<Integer> findfactor(int number) {
        ArrayList<Integer> factors= new ArrayList<>();
        for (int i = 1; i <= number; i++) {
            if (number % i == 0) {
                factors.add(i);
            }
        }
        return factors;
    }
}
```

In the preceding code, we used the brute force method, which divides the specified number by all numbers less than or equal to the number. If the number is divisible, then the divisor is added to the list of factors. We can use this with a `map` operator, which is shown in the following code:

```
fibonacciGenerator.skip(1).take(10).map(t->
numberConvertor.findfactor(t.intValue())).subscribe(t -> {
    System.out.println(t);
});
```

The resulting output includes individual collections that contain factors of the Fibonacci number:

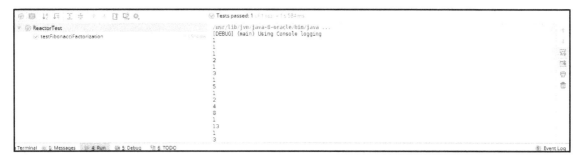

In order to make the generated factors a stream of integral factors, we must use the `flatMap` operator. This is shown in the following code:

```
Factorization numberConvertor= new Factorization();
fibonacciGenerator.skip(1).take(10).flatMap(t->
Flux.fromIterable(numberConvertor.findfactor(t.intValue()))).subscribe(t ->
{
    System.out.println(t);
});
```

In the preceding code, the following things are handled:

- `flatMap` takes an integer and passes it to the factor generator. It expects a publisher of the other data type.
- Factors are generated as a collection of integers.
- These integers are converted into a Flux using the `fromIterable` methods to match the expectations of the `FlatMap` method.

The preceding code generates the following output:

When using `flatMap`, it is essential to know what kind of Flux we are generating back. A simple change from `Flux.fromIterable` to `Flux.just` alters the complete behavior of the preceding code.

The repeat operator

Reactor provides an operator to replay a stream of data. The `repeat` operator is designed for this purpose. It replays the steam upon receiving the completion event. Let's suppose that we want to output the Fibonacci series twice. We will use the `repeat()` operator, with 2 as the argument to the `repeat()` operator:

```
fibonacciGenerator.take(10).repeat(2).subscribe(t -> {
    System.out.println(t);
});
```

The preceding code generated the stream twice, as shown in the following output. It is important to note that the `repeat()` operator repeats a stream after receiving the completion event:

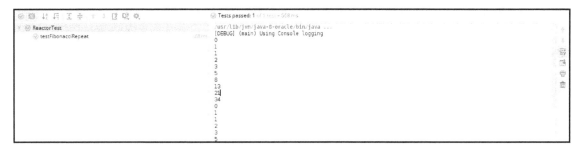

Reactor also makes it possible to perform infinite repeats. The `repeat()` operator, invoked without any argument, replays the stream an infinite number of times:

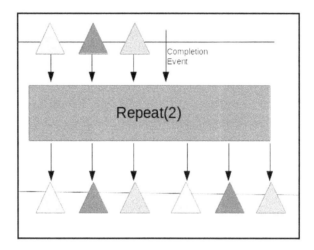

There is also a predicate variant in which a Boolean provider is passed to the repeat operator. Upon completion, the provider is evaluated every time in order to discover whether the stream needs to be repeated.

The collect operator

Reactor also provides operators that make it possible to accumulate data streams as collections. The most basic of these is the `collectList()` operator. The operator accumulates the data as a list, as shown in the following diagram:

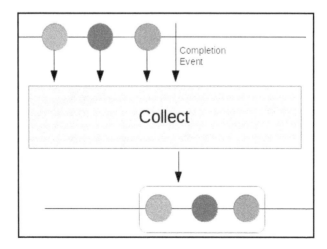

Let's take our Fibonacci example and collect the data into a list. The collector method provides a Mono publisher that will emit a single list containing all of the published data:

```
public void testFibonacciCollect() {
    Flux<Long> fibonacciGenerator = Flux.generate(
            () -> Tuples.<Long, Long>of(0L, 1L),
            (state, sink) -> {
                sink.next(state.getT1());
                return Tuples.of(state.getT2(), state.getT1() +
state.getT2());
            });
        fibonacciGenerator.take(10).collectList().subscribe(t -> {
            System.out.println(t);
        });
}
```

The preceding code performs the following actions:

- The `take` operator selects the first 10 elements of the stream
- It then accumulates them into a list, giving back a Mono publisher
- The list is provided to the subscriber, which prints it to the console

The behavior is confirmed in the following output:

The `collectList()` operator aggregates the data in a list, but there is also a `CollectSortList` operator, which can collect data in a sorted list based on the natural order of the data. We can also provide a comparator to the `CollectSortedList` method to alter the order of the data, as shown in the following code:

```
fibonacciGenerator.take(10).
collectSortedList((x,y)-> -1*Long.compare(x,y))
.subscribe(t -> {
    System.out.println(t);
});
```

The preceding code performs the following actions:

- The `take` operator selects the first 10 elements of the stream
- It then accumulates them into a `SortedList` by using the passed comparator function, giving back a Mono publisher
- The comparator function compares two long data types and reverses the evaluation
- The list is provided to the subscriber, which prints it to the console

Here, the subscriber receives a list in the reverse order of the data:

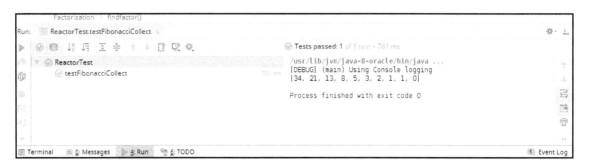

The collectMap operator

Just like `collectlist()`, Reactor also provides `collectMap()` to accumulate data into a `java.util.Map`; `collectMap` takes a key generator function to create keys for the generated value elements. This is shown in the following code:

```
fibonacciGenerator.take(10)
.collectMap(t -> t%2==0 ? "even": "odd")
.subscribe(t -> {
    System.out.println(t);
});
```

The preceding code generates a `Map` with two keys that are represented as `even` and `odd`. It will keep the last even/odd number in the map. This is shown as follows:

The `collectMap` command not only takes a `keyGeneator`, but also provides the option to pass a value generator. The value generator alters the original value of the data stream.

There is also a `CollectMultiMap()` method, which collects data into a map of keys and lists them as values. Instead of overwriting the original value, it aggregates the values against the same key into a list. If executed with the `collectMultiMap` operator, the preceding code produces the following output:

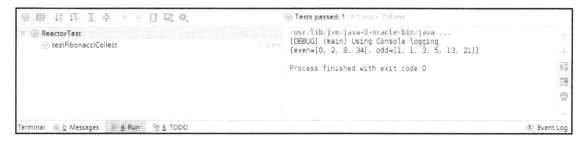

In addition to the accumulators discussed previously, there is a generic `Collect` operator, which makes it possible to accumulate data into any format. This operator converts the Flux publisher back to a Mono publisher, emitting a single accumulated value.

The reduce operator

The preceding section covered value accumulation, whereas the reduce operation revolves around value consolidation. The reduce method makes it possible to aggregate the complete data stream into a single value. This is depicted as follows:

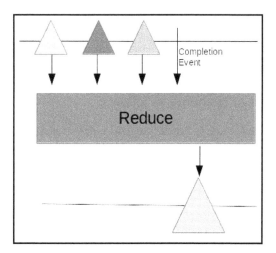

Suppose that we want to generate a sum of Fibonacci numbers, as follows:

```
fibonacciGenerator.take(10).reduce((x,y) -> x+y).subscribe(t -> {
    System.out.println(t);
});
```

In the preceding code, we did the following things:

- The `take` operator selected the first 10 elements for the stream.
- The `reduce` operator took a Bifunction of the long type. The lambda expression returns the sum of the long values to generate the back sum.
- The `subscribe` operation received a `Mono<Long>`, which was printed on the console. This is depicted as follows:

There is also an overloaded `reduce` method, which can take an initial value as the starting point of the aggregation.

There is a special `count` operator that is responsible for returning the size of the stream.

Conditional tests

Until now, we been discussed operators that work on original data. The Reactor framework provides Boolean operators that enable the testing of each of the data elements in the stream. There are two types of operators, as follows:

- `all`: This operator takes a predicate and confirms whether all of the elements meet the specified criteria. This is the logical AND operator for all data elements.
- `any`: This operator takes a predicate and confirms whether any single element meets the specified criteria. This is a logical OR for all data elements.

The results of the preceding methods are consolidated into a single Boolean result, as follows:

```
fibonacciGenerator.take(10).all(x -> x > 0).subscribe(t -> {
    System.out.println(t);
});
```

In the preceding code, we did the following things:

- The `take` operator selected the first `10` elements for the stream.
- The `all` operator took a Boolean predicate to confirm that all of the elements are greater than `0`.
- The `subscribe` operation received a `Mono<Boolean>`, which was printed on the console.

The output is as follows:

Appending data

Until now, we have worked on data generated from a single Flux stream. Stream processing is not limited to one publisher. Reactor provides operators that make it possible to merge different publishers into one single stream of data. Values can be added either before the specified published values or after the published values.

The concatWith operator

The `concatWith` operator makes it possible to append a value event after the published values. It takes a publisher as input and appends the published values after the first publisher has completed, as shown in the following diagram:

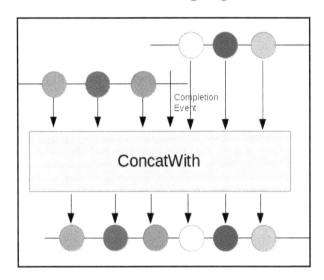

Let's suppose that we want to append some negative values at the end of our Fibonacci stream:

```
fibonacciGenerator.take(10)
  .concatWith(Flux.just( new Long[]{-1L,-2L,-3L,-4L}))
  .subscribe(t -> {
    System.out.println(t);
});
```

In the preceding code, we did the following things:

- The `take` operator selected the first 10 elements for the stream.
- The `concatWith` operator took a publisher. It appended its values after the completion of the original stream, that is, after 10 elements.
- The `subscribe` operation received a `Flux<Long>`, which was printed on the console.

Similar to `concatWith`, there is a `startWith` operator, which can be used to add values before the original stream values.

Summary

In this chapter, we discussed the wide range of operators available in Reactor. We started by looking at simple operators for selecting and rejecting data. We then looked at operators for converting data to other types. The converted data element does not need to be one-to-one mapped. There can be more than one element for each processed value. Next, we looked at operators that accumulate data. By the end of the chapter, we had covered aggregation and conditional tests for data. In a nutshell, we have covered the complete range of operators available in Reactor. In the next chapter we will look at the processors, which provide the necessary glue to bind Reactor components.

Questions

1. What operator is used to select data elements from a stream?
2. What operator is used to reject data elements from a stream?
3. What operators does Reactor offer for data conversion? How are these operators different from each other?
4. How can we perform data aggregation by using Reactor operators?
5. What conditional operators are offered by Reactor?

4
Processors

So far in this book, we have been covering the building blocks of Reactive Streams. The publisher, subscriber, and operators represent data manipulation components. Processors, on the other hand, represent the plumbing required to join these components into a single stream of data. In this chapter, we will discuss the types and requirements of processors in detail.

The following topics will be covered in this chapter:

- An introduction to processors
- Understanding processor types
- Hot versus cold publishers

Technical requirements

- Java Standard Edition, JDK 8 or above
- IntelliJ IDEA IDE, 2018.1 or above

The GitHub link for this chapter is `https://github.com/PacktPublishing/Hands-On-Reactive-Programming-with-Reactor/tree/master/Chapter04`.

An introduction to processors

A processor represents a state of data processing. It is therefore presented as both a publisher and a subscriber. Since it is a publisher, we can create a processor and `Subscribe` to it. Most of the functions of a publisher can be performed using a processor; it can inject custom data, as well as generate errors and completion events. We can also interface all operators on it.

Consider the following code:

```
DirectProcessor<Long> data = DirectProcessor.create();
data.take(2).subscribe(t -> System.out.println(t));
data.onNext(10L);
data.onNext(11L);
data.onNext(12L);
```

In the preceding code, we did the following things:

1. We added an instance of `DirectProcessor`
2. In the second line, we added the `take` operator, to select two elements
3. We also subscribed and printed the data on the console
4. In the last three lines, we published three data elements

Let's take a look at the output, as shown in the following screenshot:

Here, it looks like we can replace the publisher with processors. But if this is the case, why did the Reactive Stream specification ask for two interfaces for the same function? Well, the publisher and processor are not actually the same. Processors are special class publishers that have limited capabilities. They represent a stage of data processing. We will familiarize ourselves with these limitations when we discuss the different types of available processors.

As a general rule, we should try to refrain from using processors directly. Instead, we should try to look for the following alternatives:

- First, determine an existing operator that can provide the intended functions. Operators should be the first choice for carrying out data manipulation.
- If there is no operator available, we should try to adapt the `Flux.generate` API and generate a custom stream of data.

Understanding processor types

There are different types of processors available in Reactor. These processors differ in various features, such as backpressure capability, the number of clients they can handle, synchronous invocation, and so on. Let's look at the types of processor available in Reactor.

The DirectProcessor type

`DirectProcessor` is the simplest of the processors. This processor connects a processor to a subscriber, and then directly invokes the `Subscriber.onNext` method. The processor does not offer any backpressure handling.

An instance of `DirectProcessor` can be created by invoking the `create()` method. Any number of subscribers can subscribe to the processor. It must be noted that once the processor has published the complete event, it will reject subsequent data events.

Consider the following code:

```
DirectProcessor<Long> data = DirectProcessor.create();
data.subscribe(t -> System.out.println(t),
        e -> e.printStackTrace(),
        () -> System.out.println("Finished 1"));
data.onNext(10L);
data.onComplete();
data.subscribe(t -> System.out.println(t),
        e -> e.printStackTrace(),
        () -> System.out.println("Finished 2"));
data.onNext(12L);
```

The preceding code does the following:

1. Creates an instance of `Directprocessor`
2. Adds a subscriber that can print all events (data/error/completion) to the console
3. Publishes a data event, followed by a completion event
4. Adds another subscriber, which can print all events (data/error/completion) to the console
5. Publishes a data event.

When we look at the following output screenshot, we can see that all subscribers get the completion event. The data event for the value of `12` then gets dropped:

With respect to the handling of backpressure, `DirectProcessor` has another important limitation. We mentioned previously that it does not have backpressure capability at all. This means that if we push events more than what is asked by the subscriber, it leads to an `Overflow` exception.

Let's look at the following code:

```
DirectProcessor<Long> data = DirectProcessor.create();
data.subscribe(t -> System.out.println(t),
        e -> e.printStackTrace(),
        () -> System.out.println("Finished"),
        s -> s.request(1));
data.onNext(10L);
data.onNext(11L);
data.onNext(12L);
```

The preceding code does the following things:

1. Created an instance of `Directprocessor`
2. Added a subscriber that can print all events (data/error/completion) to the console
3. The subscriber also listened to the subscription event and raised a demand of `1` data event
4. Finally, a couple of data events were published

The preceding code failed, displaying the following error:

The UnicastProcessor type

The `UnicastProcessor` type is like the `DirectProcessor`, in terms of invocations of the `Subscriber.onNext` method. It invokes the subscriber method directly. However, unlike the `DirectProcessor`, the `UnicastProcessor` is capable of backpressure. Internally, it creates a queue to hold undelivered events. We can also provide an optional external queue to buffer the events. After the buffer is full, the processor starts to reject elements. The processor also makes it possible to perform cleanup for every rejected element.

The `UnicastProcessor` provides `create` methods to build an instance of the processor. Let's take a look at the following code to see how this is used:

```
UnicastProcessor<Long> data = UnicastProcessor.create();
data.subscribe(t -> {
    System.out.println(t);
});
data.sink().next(10L);
```

The preceding code did the following things:

1. Created an instance of `UnicastProcessor`
2. Added a subscriber, which can print data events to the console
3. Created a `sink` to push a couple of elements

While `UnicastProcessor` provides backpressure capability, a major limitation is that only a single subscriber can be worked with. If we add one more subscriber to the preceding code, it will fail with the following error:

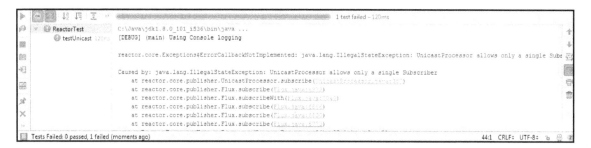

 Each processor provides a `Sink` method. A `Sink` is the preferred way of publishing events to the subscriber. It provides methods to publish next, error, and complete events. `Sink` provides a thread-safe manner of handling these events, instead of directly publishing them by using the `Subsciber.OnNext` method calls.

The EmitterProcessor type

`EmitterProcessor` is a processor that can be used with several subscribers. Multiple subscribers can ask for the next value event, based on their individual rate of consumption. The processor provides the necessary backpressure support for each subscriber. This is depicted in the following diagram:

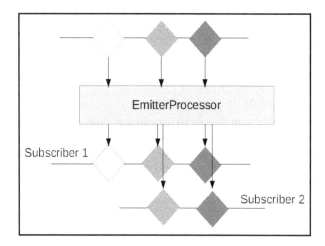

The processor is also capable of publishing events from an external publisher. It consumes an event from the injected publisher and synchronously passes it to the subscribers.

Let's look at the following code:

```
EmitterProcessor<Long> data = EmitterProcessor.create(1);
data.subscribe(t -> System.out.println(t));
FluxSink<Long> sink = data.sink();
sink.next(10L);
sink.next(11L);
sink.next(12L);
data.subscribe(t -> System.out.println(t));
sink.next(13L);
sink.next(14L);
sink.next(15L);
```

The preceding code did the following:

1. Created an instance of `EmitterProcessor`
2. Added a subscriber, which can print data events to the console
3. Created a `sink` to push a couple of elements
4. Added another subscriber, which can print data events to the console
5. Pushed more events by using the Sink API

The preceding code builds the following output:

The preceding code also made the following clear:

- Both subscribers print items to the console.
- The processor delivers events to a subscriber after its subscription. This is different from Flux, which delivers all items to all subscribers, irrespective of the time of subscription.

The ReplayProcessor type

ReplayProcessor is a special-purpose processor, capable of caching and replaying events to its subscribers. The processor also has the capability of publishing events from an external publisher. It consumes an event from the injected publisher and synchronously passes it to the subscribers.

ReplayProcessor can cache events for the following scenarios:

- All events
- A limited count of events
- Events bounded by a specified time period
- Events bounded by a count and a specified time period
- The last event only

Once cached, all events are replayed when a subscriber is added:

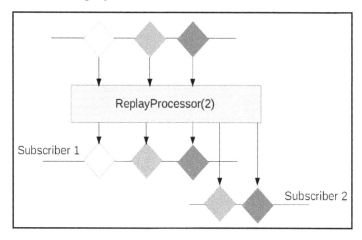

Let's look at the following code:

```
ReplayProcessor<Long> data = ReplayProcessor.create(3);
data.subscribe(t -> System.out.println(t));
FluxSink<Long> sink = data.sink();
sink.next(10L);
sink.next(11L);
sink.next(12L);
sink.next(13L);
sink.next(14L);
data.subscribe(t -> System.out.println(t));
```

The preceding code did the following things:

1. Created an instance of `ReplayProcessor`, with a cache of three events
2. Added a subscriber, which can print data events to the console
3. Created a `sink` to push a couple of elements
4. Added another subscriber, which can print data events to the console

The preceding code builds the following output:

- The processor caches the last three events, namely, `12`, `13`, and `14`
- When the second subscriber connects, it prints the cached events on the console

A screenshot of the output is as follows:

The TopicProcessor type

`TopicProcessor` is a processor capable of working with multiple subscribers, using an event loop architecture. The processor delivers events from a publisher to the attached subscribers in an asynchronous manner, and honors backpressure for each subscriber by using the `RingBuffer` data structure. The processor is also capable of listening to events from multiple publishers. This is illustrated in the following diagram:

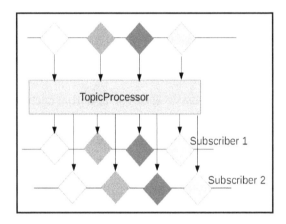

Unlike the processors that deliver events in an ordered manner, `TopicProcessor` is capable of delivering events to subscribers in a concurrent manner. This is governed by the number of threads created in the processor.

Let's look at the following code:

```
TopicProcessor<Long> data = TopicProcessor.<Long>builder()
        .executor(Executors.newFixedThreadPool(2)).build();
data.subscribe(t -> System.out.println(t));
data.subscribe(t -> System.out.println(t));
FluxSink<Long> sink= data.sink();
sink.next(10L);
sink.next(11L);
sink.next(12L);
```

The preceding code did the following things:

1. Created an instance of `TopicProcessor` by using the provided builder
2. Provided a `ThreadPool` of size 2, in order to connect two subscribers to it
3. Added two subscriber instances, which can print data events to the console
4. Created a `sink` to push a couple of elements

The preceding code builds the following output, and the processor delivers events to both subscribers concurrently:

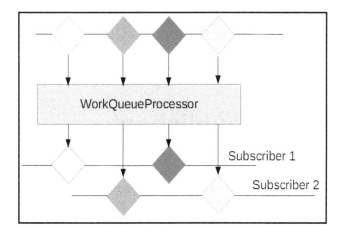

The WorkQueueProcessor type

The `WorkQueueProcessor` type is similar to the `TopicProcessor`, in that it can connect to multiple subscribers. However, it does not deliver all events to each subscriber. The demand from every subscriber is added to a queue, and events from a publisher are sent to any of the subscribers. The model is more like having listeners on a JMS queue; each listener consumes a message when finished. The processor delivers messages to each of the subscribers in a round-robin manner. The processor is also capable of listening to events from multiple publishers. This is depicted in the following diagram:

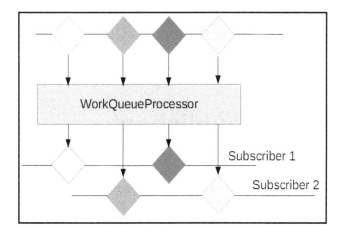

The processor is better in terms of resource requirements, as it does not build a thread pool for its subscribers.

Let's look at the following code:

```
WorkQueueProcessor<Long> data = WorkQueueProcessor.<Long>builder().build();
data.subscribe(t -> System.out.println("1. "+t));
data.subscribe(t -> System.out.println("2. "+t));
FluxSink<Long> sink= data.sink();
sink.next(10L);
sink.next(11L);
sink.next(12L);
```

The preceding code did the following things:

1. Created an instance of `WorkQueueProcessor` by using the provided builder.
2. Added two subscriber instances, which can print data events to the console. Each subscriber prints its ID, as well.
3. Created a `sink` to push a couple of elements.

The preceding code builds the following output. The processor delivers a few events to the first subscriber, with the rest being delivered to the second subscriber:

Hot versus Cold publishers

In previous chapters, we built publishers that would start publishing data to each of the subscriber instances after subscription. The Fibonacci publisher that we created in Chapter 2, *The Publisher and Subscriber APIs in a Reactor*, would publish the complete Fibonacci series to each of its subscribers.

Consider the following Fibonacci code as a cold publisher:

```
Flux<Long> fibonacciGenerator = Flux.generate(
        () -> Tuples.<Long, Long>of(0L, 1L),
        (state, sink) -> {
```

```
            sink.next(state.getT1());
            return Tuples.of(state.getT2(), state.getT1() +
state.getT2());
        });

    fibonacciGenerator.take(5).subscribe(t -> System.out.println("1. "+t));
    fibonacciGenerator.take(5).subscribe(t -> System.out.println("2. "+t));
```

Publishers that start publishing data to the subscriber after subscription are known as **cold publishers**. It is important to understand that the data should be generated post-subscription. If there is no subscriber, then the publisher will not generate any data.

Let's take a look at the output of the preceding cold publisher. Here, both subscribers print the complete set of Fibonacci numbers:

In the current chapter, we have used the processors as publishers, which do not depend on the subscriber. These publishers keep emitting data, and, when a new subscriber arrives, it receives only newly emitted data. This is different from cold publisher behavior, which also publishes old data for every new subscriber. These publishers are known as **hot publishers**.

In the following code, we have converted a Fibonacci publisher into a hot publisher:

```
final UnicastProcessor<Long> hotSource = UnicastProcessor.create();
final Flux<Long> hotFlux = hotSource.publish().autoConnect();
hotFlux.take(5).subscribe(t -> System.out.println("1. " + t));
CountDownLatch latch = new CountDownLatch(2);
new Thread(() -> {
    int c1 = 0, c2 = 1;
    while (c1 < 1000) {
        hotSource.onNext(Long.valueOf(c1));
        int sum = c1 + c2;
        c1 = c2;
        c2 = sum;
        if(c1 == 144) {
            hotFlux.subscribe(t -> System.out.println("2. " + t));
```

```
            }
        }
        hotSource.onComplete();
        latch.countDown();
    }).start();
    latch.await();
```

The preceding code illustrates the following:

1. We built a `UnicastProcessor` and converted it to a `Flux` by using the `publish` method
2. We then added a subscriber to it
3. Next, we created a `Thread` and used the `UnicastProcessor` instance (created previously) to generate the Fibonacci series
4. Another subscriber is added when the series value is `144`

Let's take a look at the output of the hot publisher:

- The first subscriber prints the initial values.
- The second subscriber prints values that are greater than `143`. This is shown in the following screenshot:

Summary

In this chapter, we explored the various kinds of processors that are available in Reactor. You learned that the `DirectProcessor` is the simplest processor, but it does not offer backpressure. We then discussed the functions and abilities of `UnicastProcessor`, `EmmiterProcessor`, `ReplayProcessor`, `TopicProcessor`, and `WorkQueueProcessor`. In the end, we familiarized ourselves with hot and cold publishers, ultimately using `UnicastProcessor` to convert a Fibonacci generator into a hot publisher.

Questions

1. What are the limitations of `DirectProcessor`?
2. What are the limitations of `UnicastProcessor`?
3. What are the capabilities of `EmitterProcessor`?
4. What are the capabilities of `ReplayProcessor`?
5. What are the capabilities of `TopicProcessor`?
6. What are the capabilities of `WorkQueueProcessor`?
7. What is the difference between a hot publisher and a cold publisher?

5
SpringWebFlux for Microservices

Up until this point, we have discussed Reactor as a standalone framework. We have also seen how we can build publishers and subscribe to them. Reactor is well suited to handling the exchanging of large volumes of data, but it is important to note that Reactor is not limited to standalone programming only; it can also be used to build web applications.

Traditionally, we built enterprise-grade web applications using the SpringMVC framework, a synchronous and blocking framework from the Spring ecosystem. SpringMVC can also serve asynchronous non-blocking data using Servlet 3.1, but then it moves away from the concepts of request mappers and filters. This makes the framework quite difficult to work with. Furthermore, when building microservice architecture for high performance, the framework may not be the optimum choice. With such an architecture, we would like to have independent, scalable, and resilient services. SpringMVC doesn't define any of these characteristics. As discussed in `Chapter 1`, *Getting Started with Reactive Streams*, the previously discussed non-functional requirements are the characteristics of the Reactive Manifesto.

Noticing this gap, the Spring community came up with the SpringWebFlux framework. This framework is based on Reactor and enables the creation of web-based microservices. Not just non-blocking, SpringWebFlux is a functional framework, which allows us to use Java 8 lambda functions as web endpoints. The framework offers a complete solution for non-blocking web stacks.

Technical requirements

- Java Standard Edition, JDK 8 or above
- IntelliJ IDEA IDE 2018.1 or above

The GitHub link for this chapter is `https://github.com/PacktPublishing/Hands-On-Reactive-Programming-with-Reactor/tree/master/Chapter05`.

Introduction to SpringWebFlux

To enable us to build web-based services, SpringWebFlux offers the following programming models:

- **Annotations**: Annotations were originally part of the SpringMVC stack. These annotations are also supported by the SpringWebFlux framework. This is the easiest way of getting started with the SpringWebFlux stack.
- **Functional endpoints**: This model allows us to build Java 8 functions as web endpoints. The application can be configured as a set of routes, handlers, and filters. It then enables passing all of these as lambda functions in order to build the application in a functional paradigm.

In order to work with SpringWebFlux, we need to configure an underlying server. While writing this book, Netty, Tomcat, Jetty, and Undertow are the choices currently offered here. Netty is often used as the standard choice because it performs well for asynchronous, non-blocking applications. It is also a non-servlet-based server, unlike Tomcat and Jetty. The following diagram depicts this:

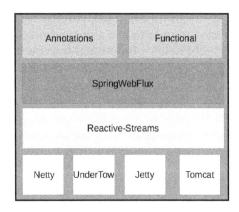

Configuring annotations

SpringWebFlux supports annotation-based controllers. This is in line with SpringMVC. There are two annotations used to create controllers:

- `@Controller`: The annotation defines a generic web component. Given a request, it creates a model object and generates a dynamic view response for it.
- `@RestController`: The annotation defines a RESTful web service. Given a request, it returns a response as JSON or XML. This is unlike the generic controller, which is capable of generating a dynamic web page for a request.

Each of the controllers serves a request pattern. The following are annotations that can be used to define the request patterns served by a controller:

- `@RequestMapping`: This annotation is used to mark a controller. It defines a request pattern prefix. It can also be used to define request headers, media types, HTTP methods, and so on.
- `@GetMapping`: This annotation is specific to the GET HTTP method. It can be used to define a GET HTTP request URL.
- `@PostMapping`: This annotation is specific to the POST HTTP method. It can be used to define a POST HTTP request URL.
- `@PutMapping`: This annotation is specific to the PUT HTTP method. It can be used to define a PUT HTTP request URL.
- `@DeleteMapping`: This annotation is specific to the DELETE HTTP method. It can be used to define a DELETE HTTP request URL.
- `@PatchMapping`: This annotation is specific to the PATCH HTTP method. It can be used to define a PATCH HTTP request URL.

It is important to note that `@RequestMapping` matches all HTTP request methods, unlike the rest of the specific method annotations.

SpringBoot Starter

Now, let's try to define a RESTful Fibonacci web service using the previously discussed annotations support. To do this, we are going to use Spring Boot as it offers a quick way to create enterprise-grade Spring applications. The Spring Boot project provides starter dependencies for all Spring modules. Each starter has assumed default conventions to ensure that a project is up and running without a fuss.

In order to use SpringWebFlux, we need to add the `spring-boot-starter-webflux` dependency to our project. Let's revisit our `build.gradle`, as shown here:

```
buildscript {
    repositories {
        maven { url 'https://repo.spring.io/libs-snapshot' }
    }

    dependencies {
        classpath 'org.springframework.boot:spring-boot-gradle-
plugin:2.0.3.RELEASE'
        compile 'org.springframework.boot:spring-boot-starter-webflux'


    }
}

apply plugin: 'org.springframework.boot'
apply plugin: 'java'
apply plugin: 'io.spring.dependency-management'
```

In the preceding `build.gradle`, we have the following changes:

1. The `spring-boot` plugin has been added to our `gradle` build.
2. The `spring-boot-dependency` plugin has been added to our `gradle` build. The plugin adds a Maven-like dependency management capability to our `gradle` build.
3. `spring-boot-starter-webflux` has been added as a dependency. This project brings in transitive dependencies for other `webflux`-related projects, such as `webflux`, `netty-core`, and so on.
4. The `spring-boot-gradle` plugin has been added under the plugins configuration. This enables us to run the Spring application from the command line using the `gradlew bootrun` command.

 By default, `Spring-boot-start-webflux` will bring a Netty dependency. If we decide to use Tomcat or any other server, we would exclude `spring-boot-starter-reactor-netty` and include said server dependency.

Adding a controller

We need to add a controller that can serve Fibonacci numbers. As discussed in the preceding sections, we need to add a class with the `@RestController` annotation. Let's look at the following controller:

```
@RestController
public class ReactiveController {

  @GetMapping("/fibonacci")
  @ResponseBody
  public Publisher<Long>fibonacciSeries() {
  Flux<Long> fibonacciGenerator = Flux.generate(() -> Tuples.<Long,
    Long>of(0L, 1L), (state, sink) -> {
    if (state.getT1() < 0)
    sink.complete();
    else
    sink.next(state.getT1());
    return Tuples.of(state.getT2(), state.getT1() + state.getT2());
  });
  return fibonacciGenerator;
  }

}
```

In the preceding class, we have done the following:

1. Added `@RestController` to the `ReactiveController` class. This enables the class as a RESTful web service:

   ```
   public class ReactiveController
   ```

2. Added `@GetMapping` to the `fibonacciSeries` method. This allows us to invoke the method on receiving a HTTP GET request for the `/fibonacci` URL.

3. It is important to note here that the `fibonacciSeries` method returns a `Flux<Long>`.

Now, we also need to add a `Main` class, which can run `SpringApplication`. The `Main` class must be annotated with `@EnableWebFlux` to ensure that the Spring context instantiates and registers SpringWebFlux-related classes. This is depicted using the following code:

```
@SpringBootApplication
@Configuration
@ComponentScan("com.sample.web")
@EnableWebFlux
```

```
public class ReactorMain {
 public static void main(String[] args){
  SpringApplication.run(ReactorMain.class, args);
 }
}
```

Run the application using the `gradlew bootrun` command. This will start the Netty server on port `8080`. Lastly, look up `http://localhost:8080/fibonacci` to receive the following result:

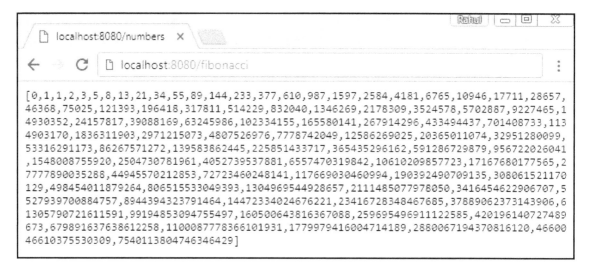

Method parameters

In the preceding code, the `fibonacciSeries` request method did not accept any arguments. This is because we did not expect any input. In case we foresee any input parameters, they can be bound with the following annotations:

- `@PathVariable`: This annotation is used to access values for URI template variables. These templates are automatically converted into an appropriate type. If no matching type is found, a `TypeMismatchException` is raised:

  ```
  @GetMapping("/contact/{deptId}/employee/{empId}")
  public Employee findEmployee(@PathVariable Long deptId,
  @PathVariable Long empId) {
  // Find the employee.
  }
  ```

- `@RequestParam`: The annotation is used to determine values passed as query parameters. Here, data type conversion is also performed automatically:

```
@GetMapping("/contact/employee")
public Employee findEmployee(@RequstParam("deptId")Long deptId,
@RequstParam("empId") Long empId) {
// Find the employee.
}
```

- `@RequestHeader`: The annotation is used to determine values passed in request headers. Data type conversion into the target type is performed automatically:

```
@GetMapping("/fibonacci")
public List<Long> fibonacci(@RequestHeader("Accept-Encoding")
String encoding) {
// Determine Series
}
```

- `@RequestBody`: The annotation is used to determine values passed in the request body. Data type conversion into the target type is performed automatically. SpringWebFlux supports reading data as reactive types of Flux and `Mono`, and thus performs a non-blocking read:

```
@PostMapping("/department")
public void createDept(@RequestBody Mono<Department> dept) {
// Add new department
}
```

- `@CookieValue`: This annotation is used to determine the HTTP cookie value as part of the request. Data type conversion into the target type is performed automatically.

- `@ModelAttribute`: This annotation is used to determine an attribute from the request model or instantiate one if not present. Once created, property values of the attribute are initialized using the query parameters passed and the submitted form fields:

```
@PostMapping("/department")
public void createdept(@ModelAttribute Department dept) {
// Add new department
}
```

- `@SessionAttribute`: This annotation is used to determine preexisting session attributes. Data type conversion into the target type is performed automatically.
- `@RequestAttribute`: This annotation is used to determine preexisting request attributes created by a previous filter execution. Data type conversion into the target type is performed automatically.

Apart from the method parameters, there is `@ResponseBody`, which is used to serialize the `return` method using the appropriate HTTP writer. This can be used to return JSON and XML type responses from the request method.

Exception handling

Applications often raise exceptions while processing requests. These exceptions must be handled properly, otherwise they will send back a HTTP 500 error to the requesting client. SpringWebFlux supports exception handling by creating methods that are annotated with `@ExceptionHandler`. These exception handlers can have the exception raised as an argument:

```
@RestController
public class ReactiveController {
 @ExceptionHandler
 public String handleError(RuntimeException ex) {
 // ...
 }
}
```

An exception handler can have the same return types as request methods. Optionally, we would like to set the HTTP status as part of exception handling, but Spring does not do this automatically. It can be accomplished by returning a `ResponseEntity`, which contains the response body as well as the required HTTP status code.

Configuring functions

In the preceding section, we configured SpringWebFlux using the traditional annotation approach. Now, we will see how we can use Java 8 lambdas to configure SpringWebFlux in a functional manner. Let's looks at the key components required to get this up and running.

The handler function

The handler function is responsible for serving a given request. It takes the request in the form of a `ServerRequest` class and generates the response as `ServerResponse`. Both `ServerRequest` and `ServerResponse` are immutable Java 8 classes. These classes support reactive types of `Mono` and Flux for reading/writing data passed in the body of the request/response. Let's try to build our first `hello-world` example using the preceding components:

```
HandlerFunction<ServerResponse> helloHandler = request -> {
        Optional<String>name=request.queryParam("name");
        return ServerResponse.ok().body(fromObject("Hello to "
+name.orElse("the world.")));
      };
```

In the preceding code, we are doing the following:

- The lambda takes a `ServerRequest` input request type
- It tries to determine whether a `name` query parameter has been passed
- The function returns the OK(HTTP 200) response
- The response body contains `Hello to the world`

This was only a simple example but it clearly demonstrates what can be accomplished using Java 8 lambdas. We can add a query to a reactive database such as Mongo, or an external invocation, and return the response as Mono or Flux. If we look closely at `ServerRequest`, the following methods have been provided to convert request-body as reactive type:

- `bodyToMono(Class<T> type)`: This reads a single object of the specified type as a Mono response
- `bodyToFlux(Class<T> type)`: This reads multiple objects of the specified type as a Flux response

If we look at the preceding code, we have used the `BodyInserters.fromObject()` static method to write to the response body. This is not the only method to do this. There are many methods to write back the response body, some of which are as follows:

- `fromObject`: This method writes back data as an object
- `fromPublisher`: This method writes back data from a given Reactive Streams publisher

- `fromFormData`: This method writes back the given key-value pair and form data
- `fromMultipartData`: This method writes back the given data as multipart data

 Handler functions written as lambdas are quite convenient but they become difficult to read and maintain in the long run. It is often recommended to group the handler functions for a particular functionality in one single handler class.

The router function

The router function is responsible for routing incoming requests to the correct handler function. If we compare this to the annotation approach, then it is analogous to the `@RequestMapping` annotation.

A request is matched using `RequestPredicate`, which tries to validate the intended matching criteria. Our previously created `helloHandler` can be configured in the following manner:

```
RouterFunction<ServerResponse> route =
RouterFunctions.route(RequestPredicates.path("/hello"),hellowHandler);
```

The preceding code is doing the following:

1. It registers a predicate for the `/hello` path
2. If a request matches this path, the router invokes `helloHandler`

If we look at `RequestPredicate`, this is a functional interface in which we need to implement the test method only:

```
public interface RequestPredicate {
  boolean test(ServerRequest var1);
  default RequestPredicate and(RequestPredicate other) {..  }
  default RequestPredicate negate() {..}
  default RequestPredicate or(RequestPredicate other) {..}
  default Optional<ServerRequest> nest(ServerRequest request) {..}
}
```

However, implementing `RequestPredicate` is not required. The framework provides the `RequestPredicates` utility class with most commonly used predicates. The utility provides routing based on HTTP methods, HTTP headers, query parameters, URL path, and so on. Let's looks at the methods offered by the `RequestPredicates` utils class:

Methods	Match
`path(String pattern)`	Predicate matches the passed URL
`patternDELETE(String pattern)`	Predicate matches the passed URL pattern when HTTP method is `DELETE`
`GET(String pattern)`	Predicate matches the passed URL pattern when HTTP method is `GET`
`PUT(String pattern)`	Predicate matches the passed URL pattern when HTTP method is `PUT`
`POST(String pattern)`	Predicate matches the passed URL pattern when HTTP method is `POST`
`PATCH(String pattern)`	Predicate matches the passed URL pattern when HTTP method is `PATCH`
`HEAD(String pattern)`	Predicate matches the passed URL pattern when HTTP method is `HEAD`
`method(HttpMethod method)`	Predicate determines if the request method is the same as that passed
`oneaccept(MediaType type)`	Predicate determines if the request accepts header contains the given `MediaType`
`contentType(mediaType type)`	Predicate determines if the request's `contentType` header contains the given `MediaType`
`headers(Predicate headerPredicate)`	Predicate determines if the request header matches the predicate query
`Param(String name, String value)`	Predicate determines if the request query parameters contain the key-value pair
`all()`	Predicate always matches the request

We can combine one or more of these predicates to build composite matching criteria. The criteria can be combined using the following methods of `RequestPredicate`:

- `RequestPredicate.and(RequestPredicate)`: Builds the logical AND criteria, where both must match
- `RequestPredicate.or(RequestPredicate)`: Builds the logical OR criteria, where either can match
- `RequestPredicate.negate()`: Builds the logical NOT criteria, which it must not match

RequestPredicates are configured using the Route functions from the RouterFunctions utility class. Additional routes can be configured using the following methods from RouterFunction:

- RouterFunctions.router(predicate,handler)
- RouterFunction.andRoute(predicate,handler)

HandlerFilter

HandlerFilter is analogous to the Servlet filter. This executes before the request gets processed by HandlerFunction. There could be chain filters that get executed before the request gets served. If a filter sends back a ServerResponse, then the request is terminated as follows:

```
helloRoute.filter((request, next) -> {
    if
(request.headers().acceptCharset().contains(Charset.forName("UTF-8"))) {
        return next.handle(request);
    }
    else {
        return ServerResponse.status(HttpStatus.BAD_REQUEST).build();
    }
});
```

The preceding code is doing the following:

1. Adding a filter to helloRoute using the filter() method
2. The filter takes a request and the next handler function
3. Validating whether or not the request headers contain the UTF-8 charset in the **Accept-Language** header
4. If so, forward the request to the next function
5. If not, then build a ServerResponse with the status as BAD_REQUEST:

```
×   Headers  Preview  Response  Timing
▼General
    Request URL: http://localhost:8080/hello
    Request Method: GET
    Status Code: ● 400 Bad Request
    Remote Address: [::1]:8080
    Referrer Policy: no-referrer-when-downgrade
▼Response Headers     view source
    content-length: 0
▼Request Headers     view source
    Accept: text/html,application/xhtml+xml,application/xml;q=0.9,image/webp,image/apng,*/*;q=0.8
    Accept-Encoding: gzip, deflate, br
    Accept-Language: en-US,en;q=0.8
    Connection: keep-alive
    Host: localhost:8080
    Upgrade-Insecure-Requests: 1
    User-Agent: Mozilla/5.0 (Windows NT 6.1; Win64; x64) AppleWebKit/537.36 (KHTML, like Gecko) Chrome/59.0.3071.115 Safari/537.36
```

HttpHandler

Now that we have mapped a request using the handler and router, the only step left is to start the server. SpringWebFlux enables us to programmatically start the server. In order to do so, we have to get `HttpHandler` from `RouterFunction` and then start the required server:

```
HttpHandler httpHandler = RouterFunctions.toHttpHandler(helloRoute);
ReactorHttpHandlerAdapter adapter = new
ReactorHttpHandlerAdapter(httpHandler);
HttpServer server = HttpServer.create("127.0.0.1", 8080);
server.newHandler(adapter).block();
```

The preceding code is specific to Netty, as we are using `reactor-netty` in our current example. In the preceding code, we are doing the following:

- Converting the `helloRoute` to a `HttpHandler` using `RoterFunctions.toHttpHandler`
- Instantiating Netty's `ReactorHttpHandlerAdapter` and using it to configure the Netty `HttpServer`
- Finally, we block to listen for incoming requests and serve them

The preceding configuration is specific to the underlying server. While working with `Undertow`, the configuration can be built using the following code:

```
HttpHandler httpHandler =  RouterFunctions.toHttpHandler(helloRoute);
UndertowHttpHandlerAdapter adapter = new
UndertowHttpHandlerAdapter(httpHandler);
Undertow server = Undertow.builder().addHttpListener(8080,
```

```
"127.0.0.1").setHandler(adapter).build();
server.start();
```

The following code is applicable to Tomcat:

```
HttpHandler httpHandler = RouterFunctions.toHttpHandler(helloRoute);
Servlet servlet = new TomcatHttpHandlerAdapter(httpHandler);
Tomcat server = new Tomcat();
File root = new File(System.getProperty("java.io.tmpdir"));
Context rootContext = server.addContext("", root.getAbsolutePath());
Tomcat.addServlet(rootContext, "ctx", servlet);
rootContext.addServletMappingDecoded("/", "ctx");
server.setHost(host);
server.setPort(port);
server.start();
```

Alternatively, we can leave all this configuration to Spring and use the Spring `DispatcherHandler`-based configuration to start the server. The configuration is Java annotation-based. The configuration automatically registers the following additional components to support functional endpoints:

- `RouterFunctionMapping`: This determines the list of `RouterFunction <?>` beans in the Spring configuration. This combines them and routes the request to the correct `RouterFunction`.
- `HandlerFunctionAdapter`: This invokes the correct `HandlerFunction` when a request is received.
- `ServerResponseResultHandler`: This writes back the `ServerResponse` from the `HandlerFunction` invocation.

All the preceding components are registered by Spring when we use the `@EnableWebFlux` annotation.

Fibonacci functional router

Now that we have seen the basics of functional mappings, let's try to render the Fibonacci series using them. We will use the same Fibonacci generator developed in the previous section. We have seen that we can write a Reactive Stream publisher into `ServerResponse`, as demonstrated in the following code snippet:

```
@Configuration
class FibonacciConfigurer {
    @Bean
    RouterFunction<ServerResponse> fibonacciEndpoint() {
        Flux<Long> fibonacciGenerator = Flux.generate(() -> Tuples.<Long,
```

```
                  Long>of(0L, 1L), (state, sink) -> {
            if (state.getT1() < 0)
                sink.complete();
            else
                sink.next(state.getT1());
            return Tuples.of(state.getT2(), state.getT1() + state.getT2());
        });
        RouterFunction<ServerResponse> fibonacciRoute =
                RouterFunctions.route(RequestPredicates.path("/fibonacci"),
                     request ->
 ServerResponse.ok().body(fromPublisher(fibonacciGenerator, Long.class)));
        return fibonacciRoute;
     }
 }
```

In the preceding code, we did the following:

1. Created a `FibonacciGenerator` to generate the series
2. Configured a route for `/fibonacci` and then sent back the response of Fibonacci numbers
3. The method is annotated with `@Bean`, which will automatically register this route with `SpringContext`
4. The class is annotated with `@Configuration`

Now, all that remains is to configure SpringWebFlux to pick this configuration. This is done by creating a `Main` class and annotating it with the required annotations:

```
@SpringBootApplication
@Configuration
@ComponentScan("com.sample.web")
@EnableWebFlux
public class ReactorMain {
    public static void main(String[] args) {
        SpringApplication.run(ReactorMain.class, args);
    }
}
```

The preceding class is exactly the same as we used to work with annotations in SpringWebFlux. Now, let's run the server using the `spring-boot` plugin:

gradlew bootrun

This brings up Netty on port `8080`. Let's submit the `http://localhost:8080/fibonacci` URL to determine the response:

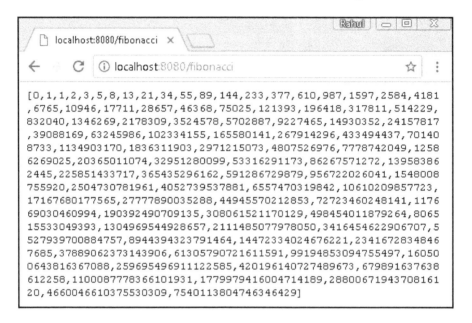

Summary

In this chapter, we looked at using the SpringWebFlux framework to build web-based microservices. We also discussed the various server options offered by the project and looked at the traditional annotation-based approach to building microservices. We discovered that all annotations from the SpringMVC project are supported by the SpringWebFlux project. Next, we took the functional approach to building microservices. We configured the router and handler functions to build the Fibonacci web service.

In the next chapter, we will look at ways to add other web features, such as web page templates, security, and much more, to a SpringWebFlux-based web service.

Questions

1. How can we configure the SpringWebFlux project?
2. What `MethodParameter` annotations are supported by SpringWebFlux?
3. What is the use of `ExceptionHandler`?
4. What is the use of `HandlerFunction`?
5. What is the use of `RouterFunction`?
6. What is the use of `HandlerFilter`?

6
Dynamic Rendering

In the last chapter, we worked with SpringWebFlux to build simple web services. So far, we have built RESTful web services, which return JSON responses. However, SpringWebFlux is not limited to RESTful web services; it is a complete web framework that offers the capability to build dynamic web pages.

In this chapter, we will discuss the following topics:

- View templates
- Static resources
- WebClient

Technical requirements

- Java Standard Edition, JDK 8 or above
- IntelliJ IDEA IDE, 2018.1 or above

The GitHub link for this chapter is `https://github.com/PacktPublishing/Hands-On-Reactive-Programming-with-Reactor/tree/master/Chapter06`.

View templates

SpringWebFlux offers a number of options for rendering views, using various technology platforms. Whatever choice we make, the framework employs the same view resolution process, allowing us to arrive at the correct view. The view can then be rendered by using any of the supported technologies. In this section, we will cover the complete process of rendering views using SpringWebFlux.

Resolving views

View resolution is a process used by the framework to determine which view needs to be rendered for a received request. The complete view resolution process enables us to render different views for the same requests, based on content parameters. Before we start to build different views, let's discuss how the framework determines what view it needs to render.

In the last chapter, we configured `HandlerFunction` for handling requests. This function gives back a `HandlerResult`. The `HandlerResult` contains not only the result, but also the attributes passed into the request. The framework then invokes `ViewResolutionResultHandler`, using the `HandlerResult`. The `ViewResolutionResultHandler` determines the correct view by validating the values returned for the following:

- **String**: If the value returned is a string, then the framework builds a view using the configured `ViewResolvers`.
- **Void**: If nothing is returned, it tries to build the default view.
- **Map**: The framework looks for the default view, but it also adds the key values returned to the request model.

The `ViewResolutionResultHandler` also looks up the content type passed in the request. In order to determine what view should be used, it compares the content type passed to the content type supported by the `ViewResolver`. It then selects the first `ViewResolver` that supports the request's content type.

It is important to note that a request can redirect to another request. In order to do this, we prefix the `redirect:` keyword before the view name. The framework then uses a `UrlBasedViewResolver` and returns a URL for redirection. If the returned URL is from the same application, then the path can be built in a relative manner (for example, `redirect:/applicationA/locationA`). If the returned URL is from an external location, then the view name can be built using an absolute URL (for example, `redirect:http://www.google.com/search/`).

Now that you know how the view resolution process works, let's try to build dynamic views by using the various supported template frameworks.

Freemarker

Freemarker is a template engine that can be used to generate dynamic HTML output. It is not limited to HTML pages; it can generate any kind of text output, such as emails, and reports. In order to use this, we have to write a template file using the Freemarker syntax. The Freemarker engine then receives the file, along with data to generate the resulting dynamic text.

Now, let's try to configure Freemarker to render our Fibonacci series. In order to use Freemarker for our view resolution, we must first add the required dependencies to our `build.gradle`, as follows:

```
plugins {
    id "io.spring.dependency-management" version "1.0.1.RELEASE"
    id "org.springframework.boot" version "2.0.3.RELEASE"
}
apply plugin: 'java'
// Rest removed for Brevity

dependencies {
        compile 'org.springframework.boot:spring-boot-starter-webflux'
        compile 'org.springframework:spring-context-support'
        compile group: 'org.freemarker', name: 'freemarker', version:
'2.3.28'
}
```

In the preceding code, we added the following:

1. `org.freemarker:freemarker`: The Freemarker template engine—at the time of writing this book, version 2.3.28 was the most recent version.
2. `spring-context-support`: This provides the required integration between Freemarker and Spring. Since we have `spring-boot` configured, we need not specify the version of the `spring-context-support` dependency.

Now that we have added Freemarker, we have to configure it. The Spring context has a view resolver registry that must be updated to include Freemarker resolver, as follows:

```
@EnableWebFlux
@Configuration
public class WebfluxConfig implements WebFluxConfigurer {

    @Override
     public void configureViewResolvers(ViewResolverRegistry registry) {
        registry.freeMarker();
    }
     @Bean
```

```
        public FreeMarkerConfigurer freeMarkerConfigurer() {
            FreeMarkerConfigurer configurer = new FreeMarkerConfigurer();
            configurer.setTemplateLoaderPath("classpath:/freemarker/");
            return configurer;
        }
    }
```

In the preceding code, we did the following:

1. Implemented the `WebFluxConfigurer` interface. The interface provides the `configureViewResolvers` method.
2. The `configureViewResolvers` is invoked by the Spring context, along with a `ViewResolverRegistry`. The registry provides the `freeMarker()` method to enable Freemarker—based resolution.
3. Next, we have to create a `FreeMarkerConfigurer`, which can set Freemarker parameters. As shown in the preceding code, we configured the template path to `classpath:/freemarker/`. This will allow us to create Freemarker templates under the path `src/main/resources/freemarker`.

Now, let's add a Freemarker template for showing the Fibonacci series. In this case, we would like to list the numbers as a simple HTML list, as follows:

```
<!DOCTYPE html>
<html>
    <head>
        <title>Reactor Sample</title>
        <meta charset="UTF-8"/>
        <meta name="viewport" content="width=device-width, initial-
scale=1.0"/>
    </head>
    <body>
        <h1>Fibonacci Numbers</h1>
        <ul style="list-style-type:circle">
        <#list series as number>
          <li>${number}</li>
        </#list>
        </ul>
    </body>
</html>
```

In the preceding HTML template, we did the following:

1. We added a `series` variable, containing a list of values.
2. The `<#list> </#list>` syntax iterates through the list, providing individual values.

3. The value is then rendered in the `<li>` HTML tag.

Now, save the file as `numbers.ftl`, under the `src/main/resources/freemarker` path.

This book does not aim to cover Freemarker syntax. To learn more about it, please refer to the official Freemarker documentation.

Now, the only configuration remaining is to use the template to render the Fibonacci series. First, let's use this template in our annotation—based controller:

```
@Controller
public class ReactiveController {

// Rest removed for Brevity
@GetMapping("/numbers")
    public String handleSeries(Model model) {
        Flux<Long> fibonacciGenerator = Flux.generate(() -> Tuples.<Long,
                Long>of(0L, 1L), (state, sink) -> {
            if (state.getT1() < 0)
                sink.complete();
            else
                sink.next(state.getT1());
            return Tuples.of(state.getT2(), state.getT1() + state.getT2());
        });
        model.addAttribute("series", fibonacciGenerator);
        return "numbers";
    }
}
```

In the preceding code, we did the following:

1. We added the `@controller` annotation, instead of `@RestContoller`. The `RestController` annotation only renders a JSON response. On the other hand, the `@controller` annotation allows us to render any kind of response.
2. We added `fibonacciGenerator(Flux<>)` to our model, as a `series` variable. This will provide the series value to the Freemarker template.
3. Next, we returned a `numbers` string as the return value. This will resolve to pick the `number.ftl` template.

Now, let's run `ReactorMain` and hit `http://localhost:8080/numbers`. At this point, we will get back an HTML page listing the Fibonacci series, as follows:

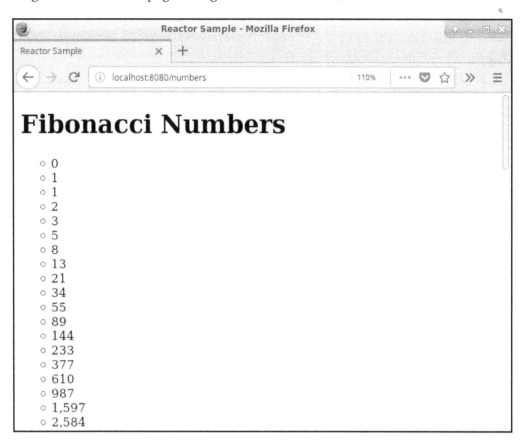

Now, let's use the Freemarker view with our `HandlerFunction`. In order to do this, we have to change `ServerResponse`, as follows:

```
@Configuration
class FibonacciConfigurer {
    // Rest removed  For Brevity
    @Bean
    RouterFunction<ServerResponse> fibonacciEndpoint() {
        Flux<Long> fibonacciGenerator = Flux.generate(() -> Tuples.<Long,
                Long>of(0L, 1L), (state, sink) -> {
            if (state.getT1() < 0)
                sink.complete();
            else
                sink.next(state.getT1());
```

```
            return Tuples.of(state.getT2(), state.getT1() +
state.getT2());
        });
        Map<String, Flux> model = new HashMap<>();
        model.put("series",fibonacciGenerator);
        RouterFunction<ServerResponse> fibonacciRoute =
RouterFunctions.route(RequestPredicates.path("/fibonacci"),
                    request ->
ServerResponse.ok().render("numbers",model));
        return fibonacciRoute;
    }
```

In the preceding code, we did the following:

- Instead of building `ServerResponse.body`, we are now using the render API. This API takes a view name and an optional map of attributes.
- We provided the series values in the map by mapping the series key to the `fibonacciGenerator` (Flux<>).

Now, let's run `ReactorMain` and hit `http://localhost:8080/fibonacci`. At this point, we will get back the same HTML page listing the Fibonacci series.

Thymeleaf

Thymeleaf is a modem template engine that is based in Java and XML/HTML. It can be used to render any XML/HTML content. Templates built with Thymeleaf are of a natural order, meaning that they will render exactly how they are designed, unlike JSPs. This template engine is aimed at replacing JSPs. It has an excellent integration with Spring.

Now, let's try to configure Thymeleaf to render the Fibonacci series. In order to use Thymeleaf for view resolution, we must first add the required dependencies to our `build.gradle`, as follows:

```
plugins {
    id "io.spring.dependency-management" version "1.0.1.RELEASE"
    id "org.springframework.boot" version "2.0.3.RELEASE"
}
apply plugin: 'java'
// Rest removed for Brevity

dependencies {
        compile 'org.springframework.boot:spring-boot-starter-webflux'
        compile "org.springframework.boot:spring-boot-starter-thymeleaf"
}
```

In the preceding code, we added the following:

- `spring-boot-starter-thymeleaf`: The Springboot starter imports the required Thymeleaf libraries. It also configures the Thymeleaf engine with predefined defaults.

Now that we have added Thymeleaf, we must enable it. The Spring context has a view resolver registry that must be updated to include the Thymeleaf resolver, as follows:

```
@EnableWebFlux
@Configuration
public class WebfluxConfig implements WebFluxConfigurer {
    private final ISpringWebFluxTemplateEngine templateEngine;

    public WebfluxConfig(ISpringWebFluxTemplateEngine templateEngine) {
        this.templateEngine = templateEngine;
    }


    @Override
    public void configureViewResolvers(ViewResolverRegistry registry) {
        registry.viewResolver(thymeleafViewResolver());
    }

    @Bean
    public ThymeleafReactiveViewResolver thymeleafViewResolver() {
        final ThymeleafReactiveViewResolver viewResolver = new
ThymeleafReactiveViewResolver();
        viewResolver.setTemplateEngine(templateEngine);
        return viewResolver;
    }


}
```

In the preceding code, we did the following:

1. Implemented the `WebFluxConfigurer` interface. This interface provides the `configureViewResolvers` method.
2. The `configureViewResolvers` method is invoked by the Spring context, along with a `ViewResolverRegistry`. We have to register a `ThymeleafReactiveViewResolver` with this.

3. `ThymeleafReactiveViewResolver` takes a
   `ISpringWebFluxTemplateEngine` engine, which is available with the Spring
   context.

4. The template engine looks for a template under
   `src/main/resources/templates`. It also adds a `.html` suffix to a template
   name before doing a lookup.

Now, let's add a Thymeleaf template to show the Fibonacci series. We would like to list the
numbers as a simple HTML list, as follows:

```
<!DOCTYPE html>

<html xmlns:th="http://www.thymeleaf.org">
    <head>
        <title>Reactor Sample</title>
        <meta charset="UTF-8"/>
        <meta name="viewport" content="width=device-width, initial-
scale=1.0"/>
    </head>
    <body>
        <section class="container">
            <ul>
                <li th:each="item : ${series}" th:text="${item}"></li>
            </ul>
        </section>
    </body>
</html>
```

In the preceding HTML template, we did the following:

1. Added a `series` variable, containing a list of values.
2. Added `<li th:each></li>`, which iterates the series variable and renders
   individual elements.

Now, save the file as `numbers.html`, under the path `src/main/resources/templates`.

> This book does not aim to cover the Thymeleaf syntax. Please refer to the
> official Thymeleaf documentation for that.

Now, the only configuration left is to use the template to render the Fibonacci series. First, let's use the template in our annotation—based controller approach:

```
@Controller
public class ReactiveController {

// Rest removed for Brevity
@GetMapping("/numbers")
    public String handleSeries(Model model) {
        Flux<Long> fibonacciGenerator = Flux.generate(() -> Tuples.<Long,
                Long>of(0L, 1L), (state, sink) -> {
            if (state.getT1() < 0)
                sink.complete();
            else
                sink.next(state.getT1());
            return Tuples.of(state.getT2(), state.getT1() + state.getT2());
        });
        model.addAttribute("series", fibonacciGenerator);
        return "numbers";
    }
}
```

In the preceding code, we did the following:

1. We added the `@controller` annotation, instead of `@RestContoller`. The `RestController` annotation only renders a JSON response. On the other hand, the `@controller` annotation can render any kind of response.
2. We added `fibonacciGenerator(Flux<>)` to our model as a series. This will provide the series value to the Freemarker template.
3. Next, we returned the `numbers` string as the return value. The returned value will map to the `number.html` template.

Now, let's run `ReactorMain` and open `http://localhost:8080/numbers`. At this point, we will get back an HTML page listing the Fibonacci series, as follows:

Now, let's use the Thymeleaf view with our `HandlerFunction`. In order to do this, we have to change `ServerResponse`, as follows:

```
@Configuration
class FibonacciConfigurer {
    // Rest removed  For Brevity
    @Bean
    RouterFunction<ServerResponse> fibonacciEndpoint() {
        Flux<Long> fibonacciGenerator = Flux.generate(() -> Tuples.<Long,
                Long>of(0L, 1L), (state, sink) -> {
            if (state.getT1() < 0)
                sink.complete();
            else
                sink.next(state.getT1());
            return Tuples.of(state.getT2(), state.getT1() +
state.getT2());
        });
        Map<String, Flux> model = new HashMap<>();
        model.put("series",fibonacciGenerator);
        RouterFunction<ServerResponse> fibonacciRoute =
RouterFunctions.route(RequestPredicates.path("/fibonacci"),
                        request ->
```

```
ServerResponse.ok().render("numbers",model));
        return fibonacciRoute;
    }
```

In the preceding code, we did the following:

- Instead of building `ServerResponse.body`, we are now using the render API. The API takes a view name and an optional map of attributes.
- We provided the series values in the map by mapping the series key to the `fibonacciGenerator (Flux<>)`.

Now, let's run `ReactorMain` and open `http://localhost:8080/fibonacci`. At this point, we will get back the same HTML page that lists the Fibonacci series.

Scripting

SpringWebFlux is also capable of using various scripting libraries for view ending. It uses the JSR-223 Java Scripting engine specification to integrate various scripting engines. At the time of writing this book, the following integrations are available:

- Handlebars, using the Nashrom engine
- Mustache, using the Nashrom engine
- React, using the Nashrom engine
- EJS, using the Nashrom engine
- ERB, using the JRuby engine
- String, using the Jython engine
- Kotlin, using the Kotlin engine

In the following section, we will cover integration with Mustache. The integrations for the other options are similar.

Mustache

Mustache is a simple template engine that is available in various languages. We will now use `Mustache.js`, the template engine in JavaScript. Mustache is often seen as logic-less, as it lacks explicit control flow statements. Control flow is achieved by using section tags.

Refer to `http://mustache.github.io/` for more details about Mustache.

Now, let's try to configure Mustache to render our Fibonacci series. We don't need any other dependencies in our `build.gradle`:

```
plugins {
    id "io.spring.dependency-management" version "1.0.1.RELEASE"
    id "org.springframework.boot" version "2.0.3.RELEASE"
}
apply plugin: 'java'
// Rest removed for Brevity

dependencies {
        compile 'org.springframework.boot:spring-boot-starter-webflux'
}
```

The Spring framework provides integration out of the box. The Spring context has a view resolver registry, which must be updated to include the `ScriptTemplate` resolver, as follows:

```
@EnableWebFlux
@Configuration
public class WebfluxConfig implements WebFluxConfigurer {

    @Override
     public void configureViewResolvers(ViewResolverRegistry registry) {
        registry.scriptTemplate();
    }

    @Bean
    public ScriptTemplateConfigurer scrptTemplateConfigurer() {
        ScriptTemplateConfigurer configurer = new
ScriptTemplateConfigurer();
        configurer.setEngineName("nashorn");
        configurer.setScripts("mustache.js");
        configurer.setRenderObject("Mustache");
        configurer.setResourceLoaderPath("classpath:/mustache/");
        configurer.setRenderFunction("render");
        return configurer;
    }


}
```

In the preceding code, we did the following:

- Implemented the `WebFluxConfigurer` interface. This interface provides the `configureViewResolvers` method.
- The `configureViewResolvers` method is invoked by the Spring context, along with `ViewResolverRegistry`. The registry provides the `scriptTemplate()` method to enable a scripting—based resolver.
- Next, we must set parameters for `ScriptTempletConfigure`. The configurer needs to enable `Mustache.js`, and evaluate it using the Nashrom engine.
- `ScriptTempletConfigure` also specifies the location of the templates. In the preceding code, we configured the location as `src/main/resources/mustache`.
- Since we are using `Mustache.js`, we also have to add `Mustache.js` (from `http://github.com/jan1/mustache.js`) under the Mustache template location.

Now, let's add a Mustache template to show the Fibonacci series. In this case, it would be beneficial to list the numbers as a simple HTML list, which is shown as follows:

```html
<!DOCTYPE html>

<html>
    <head>
        <title>Reactor Sample</title>
        <meta charset="UTF-8"/>
        <meta name="viewport" content="width=device-width, initial-
scale=1.0"/>
    </head>
    <body>
        <section class="container">
            {{#series}}
            <div class="row">
                {{.}}
            </div>
            {{/series}}
        </section>
    </body>
</html>
```

In the preceding HTML template, the following has occurred:

1. There is a `series` variable, containing a list of values.
2. The `{{#series}}` `{{/series}}` syntax iterates through the list, providing individual values.
3. The value is then rendered by using the `{{.}}` syntax in an HTML ?div> tag.

Now, save the file as `numbers.html`, under the `src/main/resources/mustache` path. The only configuration left is to use the `numbers.html` template to render the Fibonacci series. First, let's use the `numbers.html` template in our annotation—based controller approach:

```
@Controller
public class ReactiveController {

// Rest removed for Brevity
@GetMapping("/numbers")
    public String handleSeries(Model model) {
        Flux<Long> fibonacciGenerator = Flux.generate(() -> Tuples.<Long,
                Long>of(0L, 1L), (state, sink) -> {
            if (state.getT1() < 0)
                sink.complete();
            else
                sink.next(state.getT1());
            return Tuples.of(state.getT2(), state.getT1() + state.getT2());
        });
        model.addAttribute("series", fibonacciGenerator);
        return "numbers.html";
    }
}
```

In the preceding code, we did the following:

- We added the `@controller` annotation, instead of `@RestContoller`. The `RestController` annotation only renders a JSON response. The `@controller` annotation, on the other hand, allows us to render any kind of response.
- We added `fibonacciGenerator(Flux<>)` to our model as a `series`. This will provide the series value to the Mustache template.
- Next, we returned the `numbers.html` string as the returned value. The returned value will map to the `number.html` template. This is unlike the previous template engines, which automatically added a suffix to the returned string value to determine the template.

Now ,let's run `ReactorMain` and hit `http://localhost:8080/numbers`. At this point, we will get back an HTML page that lists the Fibonacci series, as follows:

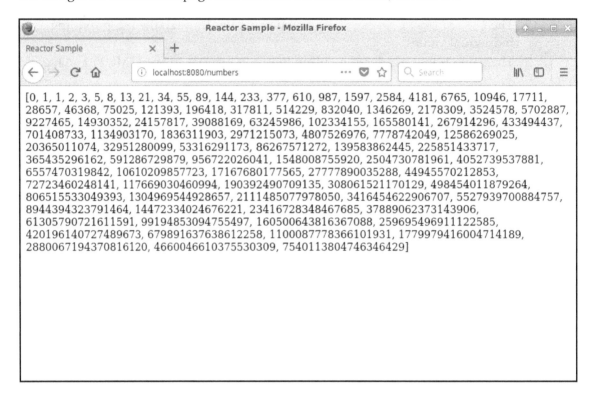

Now, let's use the Mustache view with our `HandlerFunction`. In order to do this, we have to change `ServerResponse`, as follows:

```
@Configuration
class FibonacciConfigurer {
    // Rest removed  For Brevity
    @Bean
    RouterFunction<ServerResponse> fibonacciEndpoint() {
        Flux<Long> fibonacciGenerator = Flux.generate(() -> Tuples.<Long,
                Long>of(0L, 1L), (state, sink) -> {
            if (state.getT1() < 0)
                sink.complete();
            else
                sink.next(state.getT1());
            return Tuples.of(state.getT2(), state.getT1() +
state.getT2());
        });
        Map<String, Flux> model = new HashMap<>();
```

```
        model.put("series",fibonacciGenerator);
        RouterFunction<ServerResponse> fibonacciRoute =
RouterFunctions.route(RequestPredicates.path("/fibonacci"),
                      request ->
ServerResponse.ok().render("numbers.html",model));
        return fibonacciRoute;
    }
```

In the preceding code, we did the following:

1. Instead of building `ServerRespose.body`, we are now using the render API. The API takes a view name and an optional map of attributes.
2. We provided the series values in the map by mapping the series key to the `fibonacciGenerator (Flux<>)`.

Now ,let's run `ReactorMain` and hit `http://localhost:8080/fibonacci`. In response, we will get the same HTML page listing the Fibonacci series.

Learning about static resources

A dynamic application often has static parts as well. SpringWebFlux also enables us to configure static resources. Let's suppose that we want to use `bootstrap.css` in our Thymeleaf application. In order to do this, we have to enable the server to determine the static content. This can be configured as follows:

```
public class WebfluxConfig implements WebFluxConfigurer {
    //Rest Removed for Brevity
    @Override
    public void addResourceHandlers(ResourceHandlerRegistry registry) {
        registry.addResourceHandler("/resources/**")
                .addResourceLocations("classpath:/static/");
    }
}
```

In the preceding code, the following has occurred:

1. The `addResourceHandler` method takes a URL pattern and configures it to be static locations which must be served by the server. In the preceding code, all of our static URLs should look like `like/resources/XXXX`.
2. The `addResourceLocations` method configures a location from which the static content must be served. In the preceding code, we have configured the location as `src/main/resources/static`.

Now, let's download `bootstrap.css` to `src/main/resources/static`. This will be served on `/resources/bootstrap.min.css`. The only thing left to do is to include the `css` in our `numbers.html` Thymeleaf template, as follows:

```
<html xmlns:th="http://www.thymeleaf.org">
    <head>
        <title>Reactor Sample</title>
        <meta charset="UTF-8"/>
        <meta name="viewport" content="width=device-width, initial-
scale=1.0"/>
        <link rel="stylesheet" href="/resources/bootstrap.min.css">
    </head>
    <body>
        <section class="container">
            <ul class="list-group">
                <li th:each="item : ${series}" th:text="${item}"
class="list-group-item"></li>
            </ul>
        </section>
    </body>
</html>
```

In the preceding code, the following has occurred:

1. The `<link rel="stylesheet"../>` will include the `css` from our server.
2. We have used a `container`, as well as `list-group` and `list-group-item` classes from Bootstrap, for our html elements.

Now, run the server and open `http://localhost:8080/numbers`. The page is now formatted with a Bootstrap grid, as follows:

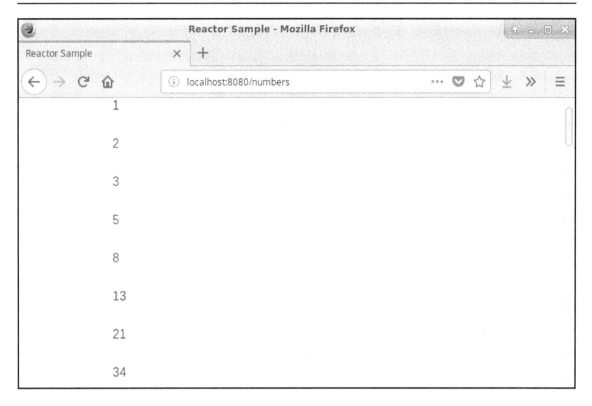

The `ResourceHandlerRegistry` also enables us to configure cache control headers. It can also be used to build a chain of resolvers that can resolve `.gz` static resources and versioned resources.

WebClient

The SpringWebFlux framework also provides a non-blocking, asynchronous HTTP client for making requests. **WebClient** offers APIs that can be configured with Java 8 lambdas, for processing data. At the backend, the WebClient API configures Netty to perform the asynchronous, non-blocking communication. Now, let's look at how we can use WebClient in our applications.

WebClient offers the following two methods for consuming data:

- `Retrieve`: This is the simplest method, which decodes the body into a Flux or Mono.
- `Exchange`: If we are interested in the response received, the `exchange` method is suited for this purpose. It provides the complete message, which can be converted back to a target type. Consider the following code for this:

```
public void readFibonacciNumbers() {
  WebClient client = WebClient.create("http://localhost:8080");
  Flux<Long> result = client.get()
          .uri("/fibonacci").accept(MediaType.APPLICATION_JSON)
          .retrieve()
          .bodyToFlux(Long.class);
  result.subscribe( x-> System.out.println(x));
}
```

In the preceding code, we built the WebClient to read the Fibonacci series response. This code achieved the following:

1. It created an instance of WebClient for the following location: `http://localhost:8080`.
2. The client makes an HTTP GET to `/fibonacci`, with the required JSON ACCEPT header.
3. It then invokes the `retrieve` method and converts the body to a `Flux<Long>`.
4. In the end, we subscribe to the Flux and print the numbers to the console.

The same Fibonacci series can be processed using the `exchange` method, as follows:

```
public void readFibonacciNumbersUsingExchange() {
    WebClient client = WebClient.create("http://localhost:8080");
    Flux<Long> result = client.get()
            .uri("/fibonacci").accept(MediaType.APPLICATION_JSON)
            .exchange()
            .flatMapMany(response -> response.bodyToFlux(Long.class));
    result.subscribe( x-> System.out.println(x));
  }
```

The following are the key differences between the `exchange` method and the `retrieve` method:

- The exchange method provides a `Mono<ClientResponse>`. This must be converted to a Flux by using the `flatMapMany` API.
- We process the response body and transform it into a `Flux<Long>`.

In addition to the differences stated in the preceding points, the retrieve method provides a convenient onStatus API. This method is used to invoke functions on the specified HTTP status code. On the other hand, in the exchange method, we get the complete response, so it is up to the developer to read the HTTP status code and invoke the required logic.

WebClient can be used to invoke HTTP GET, PUT, POST, DELETE, PATCH, and HEAD methods. When using POST, we often have to add a request body. This is done by invoking the body() API, available with the PUT method. The API takes a Mono or a Flux of a specified type. Alternatively, if there is an object available, it can be processed by using the syncBody() method. The WebClient API also offers the following methods to configure a request:

- accepts: Configures the accepts request header with the specified content type
- acceptCharset: Configures the accepts-charset request header
- header(s): Configures the specified header(s) with the specified value(s)
- attributes: Adds the specified attributes to the request
- cookies: Adds a cookies header to the request

The WebClient also provides a builder, which can be used to build a WebClient for the settings provided. This can be used to instantiate a client as a specific SSL context, or with default headers. The builder configuration is applied to the created instance of WebClient, and is thus invoked for every call we make using the instance.

SpringWebFlux also provides WebTestClient, which is an extension of WebClient, along with assertions to validate the response body and response status. The class can be instantiated in a manner similar to WebClient. After making a request using the exchange method, the response can be asserted by using the following methods:

- expectStatus(): This method can validate response status codes, such as OK and NOT_FOUND.
- expectHeader(): This method can validate response headers, such as MediaType.
- expectBody(class): This method can validate whether the response body can be converted to a specified class.
- expectBodyList(class): This method can validate whether the response body can be converted to a list of specified class objects. Post conversion, it can validate the list size and the list objects.

`WebTestClient` can be used to test and validate a `SpringWebFlux` application. `WebTestClient` provides different `bindXXX` methods, which can be used to configure a `WebTestClient` for an `ApplicationContext`, URL, controller, router function, and so on. It can then perform invocations against the configured resource, and validate the response.

Summary

In this chapter, we discussed how to render dynamic content, using the various template engines available with SpringWebFlux. We integrated Java-based template engines, Freemarker, and Thymeleaf. We also looked at how to enable a scripting-based engine, and how to work with Mustache.js. Next, we looked at serving static content by using `SpringWebFlux`. In the end, we discussed using WebClient to make asynchronous, non-blocking HTTP requests. We are now generating events and processing them. In the next chapter we will discuss ways to perform flow-control and backpressure.

Questions

1. How does the `SpringWebFlux` framework resolve a view?
2. What components are configured to use the Thymeleaf template engine?
3. What API is used to configure static resources in SpringWebFlux?
4. What are the benefits of WebClient?
5. What is the difference between the retrieve and exchange WebClient APIs?

Flow Control and Backpressure 7

In previous chapters, we have discussed how Reactor offers effective controls to check the production rate. This mechanism is often called backpressure. However, there are instances where backpressure is not an efficient strategy. In such cases, Reactor offers a number of flow control optimizations that can be used without backpressure.

In this chapter, we will cover the following topics regarding flow control and backpressure:

- GroupBy
- Buffer
- Window
- Sample
- Backpressure

Technical requirements

- Java Standard Edition, JDK 8 or above
- IntelliJ IDEA IDE 2018.1 or above

The GitHub link for this chapter is `https://github.com/PacktPublishing/Hands-On-Reactive-Programming-with-Reactor/tree/master/Chapter07`.

Flow control

Flow control is all about managing the rate of events so that a producer does not overwhelm its subscribers when raising a large number of events. A fast producer will push many events to its subscribers. Each of the subscribers will process these events as it receives them, one at a time. This sequential process can be quite inefficient, as each event is delivered over a wire.

In order to improve the efficiency, there are operators in Reactor that allow the producer to raise events in chunks. Each chunk of events is delivered to the subscriber, allowing them to work on many events simultaneously.

The groupBy operator

The `groupBy()` operator converts the `Flux<T>` into batches. The operator associates a key with each element of the `Flux<T>`. It then groups elements that have the same key. These groups are then emitted by the operator. This is depicted in the following diagram:

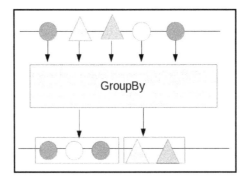

It is important to note that elements may lose their original sequence order once they are grouped. The order is enforced by the logic of the key generation. Since each element is only associated with one key, the generated groups are not empty. All the generated groups are disjointed by nature. Let's try to generate some groups for our Fibonacci series:

```
@Test
public  void testGrouping(){
    Flux<Long> fibonacciGenerator = Flux.generate(() -> Tuples.<Long,
            Long>of(0L, 1L), (state, sink) -> {
        if (state.getT1() < 0)
            sink.complete();
        else
            sink.next(state.getT1());
        return Tuples.of(state.getT2(), state.getT1() + state.getT2());
    });
    fibonacciGenerator.take(20)
            .groupBy(i -> {
                List<Integer> divisors= Arrays.asList(2,3,5,7);
                Optional<Integer> divisor = divisors.stream().filter(d
-> i % d == 0).findFirst();
                return divisor.map(x -> "Divisible by
"+x).orElse("Others");
```

```
    })
    .concatMap(x -> {
        System.out.println("\n"+x.key());
        return x;
    })
    .subscribe(x -> System.out.print(" "+x));
}
```

In the preceding code, we have carried out the following steps:

1. We partitioned the original dataset into groups of `Divisible by 2`, `Divisible by 3`, `Divisible by 5`, `Divisible by 7`, and so on.

2. `groupBy` is emitted these partitioned datasets as a key-value pair. The key is a string and the value is `List<Long>`.

3. The datasets were combined using the `concatMap` operator. We also printed the key using the operator.

4. Finally, we printed the `List` in the `Subscribe` function.

Let's run our test case to confirm the output:

The buffer operator

The `buffer()` operator gathers all `Flux<T>` elements and emits them as a `List<T>`. Unlike groups generated by the `groupBy()` operator, all the elements in the `List<T>` buffer are in their original order. Alternatively, we could provide a `batchSize` to the operator. The operator will then generate *N* lists, each of which will have a specified number of elements. Let's try to use the buffer operator on our Fibonacci series:

```
@Test
public  void testBufferWithDefinateSize(){
```

```java
Flux<Long> fibonacciGenerator = Flux.generate(() -> Tuples.<Long,
        Long>of(0L, 1L), (state, sink) -> {
    if (state.getT1() < 0)
        sink.complete();
    else
        sink.next(state.getT1());
    return Tuples.of(state.getT2(), state.getT1() + state.getT2());
});
fibonacciGenerator.take(100)
        .buffer(10)
        .subscribe(x -> System.out.println(x));
}
```

In the preceding code, we have done the following:

1. We partitioned the original dataset into buffer lists of 10 elements each
2. We then printed the list using the `subscribe` function

Let's run our test case to confirm the output. We can see that the Fibonacci elements are emitted in a single `List<Long>`:

There are many variants of the `buffer()` operator. Let's look at a few of them. Each of these generates multiple list buffers.

The `buffer(maxSize, skipSize)` operator takes two arguments. The first argument is the max size of each buffer. The second argument is the number of elements that must be skipped before starting a new buffer. The buffer lists generated by the operator have the following characteristics:

- If the `maxSize` is larger than the `skipSize`, the buffers are overlapping in nature. The next buffer starts from the element at the position specified by the `skipSize` of the previous buffer. This means that elements are duplicated across all buffers.

- If the `maxSize` is smaller than the `skipSize`, the buffers are disjointed in nature. The generated lists miss elements from the original `Flux<T>`.

- If the `skipSize` is 0, then all lists are disjointed in nature. They do not miss any elements from the original `Flux<T>`. Consider the following code:

```
@Test
public  void testBufferSizes(){
    Flux<Long> fibonacciGenerator = Flux.generate(() -> Tuples.<Long,
            Long>of(0L, 1L), (state, sink) -> {
        if (state.getT1() < 0)
            sink.complete();
        else
            sink.next(state.getT1());
        return Tuples.of(state.getT2(), state.getT1() + state.getT2());
    });
    fibonacciGenerator.take(100)
            .buffer(2,5)
            .subscribe(x -> System.out.println(x));
}
```

In the preceding code, we have done the following:

1. We partitioned the original dataset into buffers of two elements each
2. Each of the buffer lists started at the fifth element, therefore dropping three elements
3. We printed the list in the `subscribe` function

Let's run the code to confirm the output. We can see that the Fibonacci elements are emitted in a single `List<Long>`:

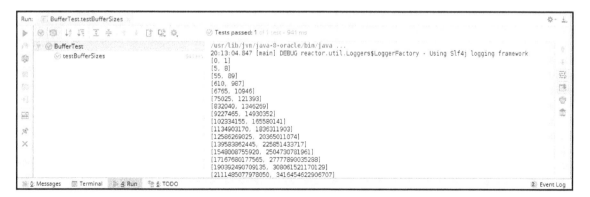

The `bufferUntil` and `bufferWhile` variants take a predicate condition and aggregate elements until the condition is true. The `bufferWhile` operator generates a single buffer that contains all elements that match the condition. On the other hand, the `bufferUntil` operator buffers non-matching elements to a list. When it finds a matching element, it adds it to the current buffer. It then starts a new buffer to add the next incoming element. This process is shown in the following diagram:

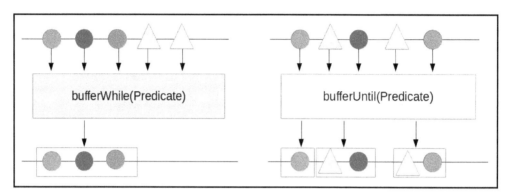

Another overloaded `buffer()` method enables us to generate buffer lists based on the time period. The operator accepts a duration and aggregates all elements during that period. It can therefore collect all events that happened during the first `Duration`, the second `Duration`, and so on, as follows:

```
@Test
public  void testBufferTimePerid(){
    Flux<Long> fibonacciGenerator = Flux.generate(() -> Tuples.<Long,
            Long>of(0L, 1L), (state, sink) -> {
        if (state.getT1() < 0)
            sink.complete();
        else
            sink.next(state.getT1());
        return Tuples.of(state.getT2(), state.getT1() + state.getT2());
    });
    fibonacciGenerator
            .buffer(Duration.ofNanos(10))
            .subscribe(x -> System.out.println(x));
}
```

In the preceding code, we have done the following:

1. We partitioned the original data based on a 10-nanosecond time slice
2. Each of the buffer lists contained elements emitted during the time period
3. Finally, we printed the lists using the `subscribe` function

Let's run this code to confirm the output. We can see that Fibonacci elements are emitted as multiple `List<Long>`:

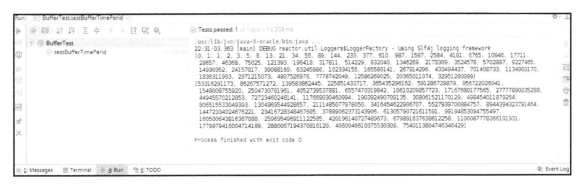

The `buffer` operator offers a number of variants of the methods discussed here. All `buffer` methods provide a list, but only one of the overloaded methods allow us to convert a buffer into a collection dataset. We need to provide a supplier function to the overloaded `buffer` operator. This function is responsible for creating a collection instance. Let's look at the following code:

```
@Test
public  void testBufferSupplier(){
    Flux<Long> fibonacciGenerator = Flux.generate(() -> Tuples.<Long,
            Long>of(0L, 1L), (state, sink) -> {
        if (state.getT1() < 0)
            sink.complete();
        else
            sink.next(state.getT1());
        return Tuples.of(state.getT2(), state.getT1() + state.getT2());
    });
    fibonacciGenerator.take(100)
            .buffer(5,HashSet::new)
            .subscribe(x -> System.out.println(x));
}
```

Here, we have done the following:

- We partitioned the original dataset into buffers of a maximum of five elements
- Each of the buffers was emitted as a `HashSet`, which means that it contains only distinct elements
- Finally, we printed the lists using the `subscribe` function

Since we used a `HashSet`, we can see that it does not contain duplicate elements of the Fibonacci series:

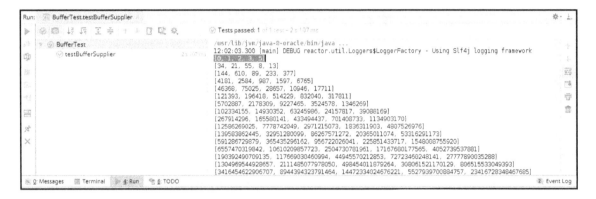

The window operator

The `window()` operator is similar to the `buffer()` operator. It also slices the original dataset, but emits each dataset as a processor, rather than as a new collection. Each processor serves as a publisher and emits items after subscribing to them. The `window` operator allows us to have a fixed window size, a time-based window, or a predicate-based window. Unlike the `buffer` operator, which allows us to build a single buffer for all published elements, the `window` operator does not allow you to publish elements in a single window.

The `window()` operator offers better memory utilization, as the items are emitted immediately rather than first being cached to a collection and then emitted once the correct collection size is achieved. The `window` operator also offers better memory usage than the buffer operator. This is depicted with the following code:

```
@Test
    public  void testWindowsFixedSize(){
        Flux<Long> fibonacciGenerator = Flux.generate(() -> Tuples.<Long,
                Long>of(0L, 1L), (state, sink) -> {
            if (state.getT1() < 0)
                sink.complete();
            else
                sink.next(state.getT1());
            return Tuples.of(state.getT2(), state.getT1() +
state.getT2());
        });
        fibonacciGenerator
                .window(10)
                .concatMap(x -> x)
                .subscribe(x -> System.out.print(x+" "));
    }
```

In the preceding code, we have done the following:

1. We partitioned the original data into windows with a maximum of 10 elements each
2. Each window is a type of `UnicastProcesser`, so it needed to be combined with the other generated windows using either `ConcatMap` or `flatMap`
3. Finally, we printed the lists using the subscribe function

Let's run this code to confirm the output. We can see that the Fibonacci elements are emitted as multiple batches and then combined as one:

The `WindowUntil` and the `WindowWhile` variants take a predicate condition and build a window batch until the condition is true. The `WindowWhile` operator generates a single window containing all the elements that match the condition. The `WindowUntil` operator, on the other hand, aggregates non-matching elements to a window. When it finds a matching element, it adds it to the current window. It then starts a new window to add the next incoming element. Consider the following code:

```
@Test
 public  void testWindowsPredicate(){
     Flux<Long> fibonacciGenerator = Flux.generate(() -> Tuples.<Long,
            Long>of(0L, 1L), (state, sink) -> {
         if (state.getT1() < 0)
             sink.complete();
         else
             sink.next(state.getT1());
         return Tuples.of(state.getT2(), state.getT1() + state.getT2());
     });
     fibonacciGenerator
             .windowWhile(x -> x < 500)
             .concatMap(x -> x)
             .subscribe(x -> System.out.println(x));
 }
```

In the preceding code, we have done the following:

1. We partitioned the original data based on the condition that `x < 500`.
2. All elements that matched the criteria were published in a single window.
3. The window elements were emitted as `WindowFlux`. They were combined using `concatMap` or `flatMap`.
4. Finally, we printed the elements with the subscribe function.

Let's run our code to confirm the output:

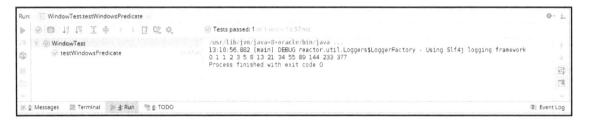

The sample operator

The `groupBy()`, `buffer()`, and `window()` operators aggregate inputs and consolidate them into chunks, based on their size, time period, or condition. They are not aimed at skipping events. At times, you may be required to skip events and listen to a particular event during a given time interval. This is often required for fast, non-changing events, such as user clicks. In such a situation, we need to throttle the flow and pick data selectively.

The `sample()` operator allows us to accomplish this throttling. It takes a time period and listens to events published during that time period. It then publishes the last event that happened during the time period. This is depicted in the following diagram:

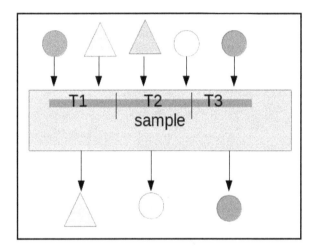

Let's try to add a delay to our Fibonacci series and then throttle it:

```
@Test
public  void testSample() throws Exception{
    Flux<Long> fibonacciGenerator = Flux.generate(() -> Tuples.<Long,
            Long>of(0L, 1L), (state, sink) -> {
        if (state.getT1() < 0)
            sink.complete();
        else
            sink.next(state.getT1());
        return Tuples.of(state.getT2(), state.getT1() + state.getT2());
    });
    CountDownLatch latch = new CountDownLatch(1);
    fibonacciGenerator
            .delayElements(Duration.ofMillis(100L))
            .sample(Duration.ofSeconds(1))
```

```
                        .subscribe(x -> System.out.println(x), e ->
    latch.countDown() , () -> latch.countDown());
            latch.await();
        }
```

In the preceding code, we have done the following:

1. We added the `delayElements()` operator. This operator is responsible for delaying each event by the supplied time period. In this case, we have delayed each element by 100 milliseconds.
2. Next, we added the `sample()` operator with a time interval of one second.
3. We then printed the elements using the `Subscribe` function.
4. We also added a `CountDownLatch` to wait for the test execution for completion/error events.

Let's run the code to confirm the output:

The `samplefirst()` operator is similar to the `sample()` operator. This operator publishes the first element that was received during the specified time period, rather than selecting the last element.

Backpressure

Backpressure is an integral part of Reactor. We have discussed it multiple times in previous chapters, but we will have a detailed look at the topic here. Let's recap the out-of-the-box support for backpressure that is available with Reactor. Each of the subscribers requests the number of events that it can process using the subscription object. The publisher must respect this limit and publish events that are less than or equal to the requested limit. This is depicted in the following diagram:

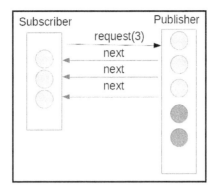

Invoking a request with `Long.MAX_VALUE` means requesting an unbounded number of events. The publisher can push as many events as it can. It is no longer bound by the subscriber limit.

As each subscriber is processing the received events, it can request additional events using the subscription handle. If the publisher is raising events rapidly, it must come up with a strategy to handle the non-requested events. Take a look at the following test code:

```
    @Test
    public void testBackPressure() throws  Exception{
        Flux<Integer> numberGenerator = Flux.create(x -> {
            System.out.println("Requested Events
:"+x.requestedFromDownstream());
            int number = 1;
            while(number < 100) {
                x.next(number);
                number++;
            }
            x.complete();
        });

        CountDownLatch latch = new CountDownLatch(1);
        numberGenerator.subscribe(new BaseSubscriber<Integer>() {
            @Override
            protected void hookOnSubscribe(Subscription subscription) {
                request(1);
            }

            @Override
            protected void hookOnNext(Integer value) {
                System.out.println(value);
            }
```

```
        @Override
        protected void hookOnError(Throwable throwable) {
            throwable.printStackTrace();
            latch.countDown();
        }

        @Override
        protected void hookOnComplete() {
            latch.countDown();
        }
    });
    assertTrue(latch.await(1L, TimeUnit.SECONDS));
}
```

In the preceding code, the following occurred:

1. We created a publisher using the `Flux.create` API
2. The publisher printed the requested number to the console and emitted 100 events
3. The subscriber requested a single event in the subscribe hook
4. The subscriber printed the received event to the console
5. There is a `CountDownLatch` to pause the code for 1 second

To sum up, the subscriber requested one event, but the publisher emitted 100. Let's run the test to see the result on the console:

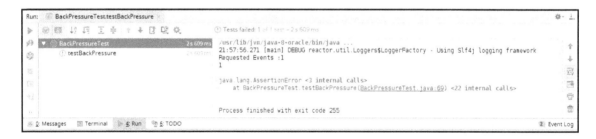

The preceding test failed to complete successfully. Our subscriber asked for one event and it received only one. The publisher, however, pushed 100 data events followed by the complete event. Reactor did some work behind the scenes to hold the events in a queue. It offers a few overflow strategies to handle events produced by a fast publisher:

Strategy	Description
IGNORE	This strategy ignores the limits of the subscriber for backpressure and keeps delivering the next event to the subscriber.
BUFFER	This strategy combines the undelivered events in a buffer. Events from the buffer are delivered when the subscriber requests the next events.
DROP	This strategy silently drops undelivered events that are produced. The subscriber will only get a newly produced event when the next request is raised.
LATEST	This strategy keeps the latest event raised in the buffer. The subscriber will only get the latest produced event when the next request is raised.
ERROR	This strategy raises an OverFlowException if the producer raises more than the events requested by the subscriber.

The API created by default uses the Overflow.Buffer strategy. We could override this by passing the one we want in the overloaded create method. Let's test the preceding code with the Overflow.Error strategy:

```
@Test
    public  void testBackPressure() throws  Exception{
        Flux<Integer> numberGenerator = Flux.create(x -> {
            System.out.println("Requested Events
:"+x.requestedFromDownstream());
            int number = 1;
            while(number < 100) {
                x.next(number);
                number++;
            }
            x.complete();
        }, OverflowStrategy.ERROR);

    // Removed for Brevity
    }
```

The test case now fails with the following error:

```
reactor.core.Exceptions$OverflowException: The receiver is overrun by more
signals than expected (bounded queue...)
    at reactor.core.Exceptions.failWithOverflow(Exceptions.java:202)
    at
reactor.core.publisher.FluxCreate$ErrorAsyncSink.onOverflow(FluxCreate.java
:632)
    at
reactor.core.publisher.FluxCreate$NoOverflowBaseAsyncSink.next(FluxCreate.j
ava:603)
    at
reactor.core.publisher.FluxCreate$SerializedSink.next(FluxCreate.java:151)
```

OnBackpressure

Reactor also provides operators to alter the overflow strategy configured with the
publisher. There are various `OnBackpressureXXX()` operators that cater to each of the
strategies available with Reactor. These are quite useful in scenarios in which none of the
preceding strategies can be applied to the publisher.

 A publisher is sometimes configured with an `IGNORE` strategy. In such
cases, backpressure is configured using operators while subscribing to the
publisher.

Let's work with our test case and apply backpressure operators to it:

```
@Test
    public  void testBackPressureOps() throws  Exception{
        Flux<Integer> numberGenerator = Flux.create(x -> {
            System.out.println("Requested Events
:"+x.requestedFromDownstream());
            int number = 1;
            while(number < 100) {
                x.next(number);
                number++;
            }
            x.complete();
        });

        CountDownLatch latch = new CountDownLatch(1);
        numberGenerator
                .onBackpressureDrop(x -> System.out.println("Dropped :"+x))
                .subscribe(new BaseSubscriber<Integer>() {
```

```
            // Removed for Brevity
        });
        assertTrue(latch.await(1L, TimeUnit.SECONDS));
    }
```

In the preceding code, we have done the following:

1. We configured `Flux<Integer>` with `OverflowStrategy.BUFFER`, the default configuration
2. While subscribing to `Flux<Integer>`, we altered the strategy to use `OverflowStrategy.DROP`
3. Additionally, we passed a lambda to the operator to print the dropped value

Let's run the code and validate the output:

Additionally, there are the `onBackpressureLatest()`, `onBackpressureError()`, and `onBackpressureBuffer()` operators, which are similar to the `onBackpressureDrop()` operator. The `onBackpressureBuffer()` operator has a couple of overloaded variants. As a basic configuration, it allows us to specify the buffer size. We could also specify one of the following strategies to handle the overflow beyond the specified buffer:

Buffer overflow	Description
`DROP_LATEST`	All generated events are buffered first and then the new events are dropped. This would keep the oldest events in the buffer.
`DROP_OLDEST`	All generated events are buffered. Events that are currently in the buffer are then replaced with new events. This would keep the latest events in the buffer.
`ERROR`	This raises an `OverFlowException` for events that are beyond the buffer.

Let's look at how this works with an example. We can also pass a consumer lambda to be invoked for the overflow events:

```
@Test
public void testBackPressureOps() throws Exception{
    Flux<Integer> numberGenerator = Flux.create(x -> {
        System.out.println("Requested Events
```

```
        :"+x.requestedFromDownstream());
                int number = 1;
                while(number < 100) {
                    x.next(number);
                    number++;
                }
                x.complete();
            });

            CountDownLatch latch = new CountDownLatch(1);
            numberGenerator
                    .onBackpressureBuffer(2,x -> System.out.println("Dropped
        :"+x),BufferOverflowStrategy.DROP_LATEST)
                    .subscribe(new BaseSubscriber<Integer>() {
            // Removed for brevity
            });
            assertTrue(latch.await(1L, TimeUnit.SECONDS));
        }
```

In the preceding code, we have done the following:

1. We configured `Flux<Integer>` with `OverflowStrategy.BUFFER`, the default configuration
2. While subscribing to `Flux<Integer>`, we altered the buffer size to two elements
3. We configured the `DROP_LATEST` strategy for events beyond the buffer
4. We also passed a lambda to the operator to print the dropped value

Let's run the code and validate the output:

Summary

In this chapter, we discussed the flow control operators that are available in Reactor in detail. We looked at the different overload options that are available in the `groupBy`, `buffer`, and `window` operators. We then considered how we can throttle events using the sample operator, which allows only a single event to be delivered in the specified time interval. After that, we recapped the support for backpressure that is available in Reactor and studied the different overflow strategies that it provides. We also learned that Reactor uses the `Overflow.Buffer` strategy by default, which can be provided as part of the `Flux.create` API. Finally, we discussed the backpressure operators that can be used to alter the strategy of the producer. To sum up, we discussed the complete list of operators available for flow control and backpressure. In the next chapter we will look at handling and recovering errors.

Questions

1. Why do we need the `groupBy` operator?
2. What is the difference between the `groupBy` and `buffer` operators?
3. How can we throttle an event in Reactor?
4. What is the difference between the `Overflow.Ignore` and `OverFlow.Latest` strategies?
5. Which operators are available to change the backpressure strategy of a producer?

8
Handling Errors

Resilience is an important aspect of reactive systems. As per the Reactive Manifesto, a reactive system must remain responsive during failure. The system must handle errors gracefully, and generate a user response in a timely manner. This cannot be accomplished without an effective error handling mechanism. Reactor offers a number of operators to handle errors. In this chapter, we will look at each of them.

In this chapter, we will cover the following topics:

- Handling errors
- Error operators
- Timeout and retry
- WebClient error handling

Technical requirements

- Java Standard Edition, JDK 8 or above
- IntelliJ IDEA IDE, 2018.1 or above

The GitHub link for this chapter is `https://github.com/PacktPublishing/Hands-On-Reactive-Programming-with-Reactor/tree/master/Chapter08`.

Generating errors

Before we try to handle errors, let's first try to raise a few. In Java ecosystems, error conditions are raised by throwing exceptions. Exceptions can be raised under the following conditions:

- The producer can throw an exception while generating the next value.
- The subscriber can throw an exception while processing the next value or subscription event, or in any operators.

In all of the preceding conditions, there must be an effective procedure for handling the error raised. Reactive Streams prescribe the error event for the same purpose. The specification states that a producer should raise an error event, instead of throwing an exception. However, the specification does not discuss exceptions raised while processing events in the subscriber. Let's start to work on our Fibonacci series, to understand how error handling happens in Reactor:

```
@Test
public void testThrownException() {
    Flux<Long> fibonacciGenerator = Flux.generate(() -> Tuples.<Long,
            Long>of(0L, 1L), (state, sink) -> {
        if (state.getT1() < 0)
            throw new RuntimeException("Value out of bounds");
        else
            sink.next(state.getT1());

        return Tuples.of(state.getT2(), state.getT1() + state.getT2());
    });
    fibonacciGenerator
            .subscribe(System.out::println);
}
```

In the preceding test case, the following occurs:

1. The generator implementation throws `RuntimeException` when the value becomes negative.
2. If we compare this to the original implementation, created in `Chapter 2`, *The Publisher and Subscriber APIs in a Reactor*, we are no longer raising a completion event.
3. There is no error function configured in the subscriber.

Let's run the test case to see how the Reactor responds, as follows:

In the preceding execution, you can see the following:

1. All positive values are first printed to the console.
2. The exception thrown is propagated to the subscriber.
3. The subscriber raises the `ErrorCallbackNotImplemented` exception, since no error function was configured.
4. The exception failed the test case.

 In the preceding test execution, please note that we did not raise an error event. However, Reactor raised the error event when the exception was thrown. The event was then handled at the subscriber end.

Now, let's enhance our test case and raise an error while processing events in the subscriber, with the following code:

```
@Test
    public void testThrownException() {
        Flux<Long> fibonacciGenerator = Flux.generate(() -> Tuples.<Long,
                Long>of(0L, 1L), (state, sink) -> {
            if (state.getT1() < 0)
                throw new RuntimeException("Value out of bounds");
            else
                sink.next(state.getT1());

            return Tuples.of(state.getT2(), state.getT1() + state.getT2());
        });
        fibonacciGenerator
                .subscribe(x -> throw new RuntimeException("Subscriber
threw error"));
    }
```

The preceding code now does the following:

1. Configures a lambda, instead of the `System.out.println` function, in the event handler.
2. The lambda throws a `RuntimeException`, instead of printing numbers to the console.

If we run the preceding test case, the output will be similar to our previous execution. The test case will fail, with the following stacktrace:

```
Caused by: java.lang.RuntimeException: Subscriber threw error
    at
ErrorHandlingTest.lambda$testThrownException$1(ErrorHandlingTest.java:16)
    at
reactor.core.publisher.FluxGenerate$GenerateSubscription.fastPath(FluxGener
ate.java:223)
    at
reactor.core.publisher.FluxGenerate$GenerateSubscription.request(FluxGenera
te.java:202)
    at
reactor.core.publisher.LambdaSubscriber.onSubscribe(LambdaSubscriber.java:8
9)
    at reactor.core.publisher.FluxGenerate.subscribe(FluxGenerate.java:83)
```

Looking at the preceding two pieces of output, we can say that Reactor handles exceptions thrown by the producer and the subscriber in the same manner. A subscriber must provide an error function to allow the Reactive Streams to finish successfully.

We have one more scenario left. Instead of throwing `RuntimeException` in the producer, we must raise an error event. This can be accomplished by replacing the `throw new RuntimeException` with `sink.error(e)`, as follows:

```
@Test
  public void testErrorRaised() {
      Flux<Long> fibonacciGenerator = Flux.generate(() -> Tuples.<Long,
              Long>of(0L, 1L), (state, sink) -> {
          if (state.getT1() < 0)
              sink.error(new RuntimeException("Value out of bounds"));
          else
              // Rest removed for Brevity
      });
  }
```

I will leave it to the reader to determine the output of the preceding test case. All of the test cases discussed have failed, due to a missing error callback handler. Consequently, we must define an error function for the subscriber. This can be accomplished by passing an additional lambda function in the `subscriber()` API. For this, consider the following code:

```
@Test
 public void testErrorRaised() {

     // Rest Removed for Brevity

     fibonacciGenerator
             .subscribe(System.out::println, System.out::println);
 }
```

In the preceding code, we have passed the `println` function in both the consumer and error consumer events. As a result, the subscriber will print both events to the console. Now, run all of our previously failing test cases; they will print the error to the console, and then finish successfully. This is shown in the following screenshot:

Checked exceptions

We cannot throw checked exceptions from the producer and the subscriber. Each of the respective Reactor methods take a `Consumer` function, without any exception declarations. So, the implementations cannot throw it. However, there are scenarios where the producer invokes resources, such as files, which can throw checked exceptions. Reactor provides the `Exceptions` utility class for handling such scenarios. The `Exceptions` class provides a `propagate` method, which can wrap any checked exception into an unchecked exception, as follows:

```
@Test
 public void testCheckedExceptions() {
     Flux<Long> fibonacciGenerator = Flux.generate(() -> Tuples.<Long,
```

```
        Long>of(0L, 1L), (state, sink) -> {
    try {
        raiseCheckedException();
    } catch (IOException e) {
        throw Exceptions.propagate(e);
    }
    return Tuples.of(state.getT2(), state.getT1() + state.getT2());
});
fibonacciGenerator
        .subscribe(System.out::println,
            e -> Exceptions.unwrap(e));
}

void raiseCheckedException() throws IOException {
    throw new IOException("Raising checked Exception");
}
```

In the preceding code, we did the following:

1. Checked that the `IOException` is thrown by the `raiseCheckedException` method
2. Used `Exception.propagate` to wrap the exception and throw it back
3. Used `Exception.unwrap` to get the original checked exception

Next, let's begin with some `try...catch` error types.

The doOnError hook

We discussed life cycle hooks in Chapter 2, *The Publisher and Subscriber APIs in a Reactor*. These can be used to configure callbacks for every life cycle event. Reactor provides the life cycle error callback hook to configure the error handler. The `doOnError` hook allows us to consume an error and perform the intended function. If we have configured the `doOnError` hook along with the error callback, then both will be invoked simultaneously by Reactor. The following code shows this:

```
@Test
public void testDoError() {
    // Removed for brevity
    fibonacciGenerator
            .doOnError(System.out::println)
            .subscribe(System.out::println, e -> e.printStackTrace());
}
```

The preceding code does the following:

1. Configures the `println` function in the `doOnError` hook. This function prints the error to the console.
2. Configures on error lambda in the subscriber API. The implementation prints the stacktrace of the thrown exception.

Let's run the preceding test case and validate the output printed on the console. Both error functions are invoked simultaneously, as follows:

The doOnTerminate hook

Similar to the `doOnError` life cycle hook, there is the `doOnTerminate` hook. This is a generic hook that is invoked for `on completion` and `on error` stream termination events. Unlike the specific error hook, which provides the exception thrown, this hook does not provide any kind of input. It just executes the lambda provided. It is important to note that the `doOnTerminate` hook is invoked as soon as we receive termination events. It does not wait for the error callback to be processed. Consider the following code:

```
@Test
public void testDoTerminate() {
    // Removed for brevity
      fibonacciGenerator
              .doOnTerminate(() -> System.out.println("Terminated"))
              .subscribe(System.out::println,e -> e.printStackTrace() );
}
```

The preceding code does the following:

1. Configures the `println` function in the `doOnTerminate` hook. This function prints `Terminated` to the console.
2. Configures an error lambda in the subscriber API. This implementation prints the stacktrace of the thrown exception.

Let's run the preceding test case and validate the output printed on the console. Both functions are invoked simultaneously, as follows:

Similar to the doOnTerminate life cycle hook, there is a doAfterTerminate life cycle hook. This hook is invoked after the close events have been delivered to the subscriber. Just like the doOnTerminate hook, doAfterTerminate is a generic hook that does not provide any events. Since the hook is invoked after the events are delivered, it requires error callback subscriber configuration. If we do not provide this, the stream fails with an ErrorCallbackNotImplemented exception.

The doFinally hook

Similar to the doOnError life cycle hook, there is the doFinally hook. This hook is invoked post-stream completion. The hook executes the lambda provided. It is important to note that the doFinally hook is invoked post-stream close callback processing, unlike the previously discussed doOnTerminate hook, which is invoked as soon as we received the close events. Consider the following code:

```
@Test
public void testDoFinally() {
    Flux<Long> fibonacciGenerator = Flux.generate(() -> Tuples.<Long,
            Long>of(0L, 1L), (state, sink) -> {
        if (state.getT1() < 0)
            sink.error(new RuntimeException("Value out of bounds"));
        else
            sink.next(state.getT1());

        return Tuples.of(state.getT2(), state.getT1() + state.getT2());
    });
    fibonacciGenerator
            .doFinally( x -> System.out.println("invoking finally"))
            .subscribe(System.out::println, e -> e.printStackTrace());
}
```

The preceding code does the following:

1. `fibonacciGenerator` raises an error on a negative value.
2. It configures the `println` function in the `doFinally` hook. The function prints `invoking finally` to the console.
3. It configures on error lambda in the subscriber API. The implementation prints the stacktrace of the thrown exception.

Let's run the preceding test case and validate the output printed on the console, as follows:

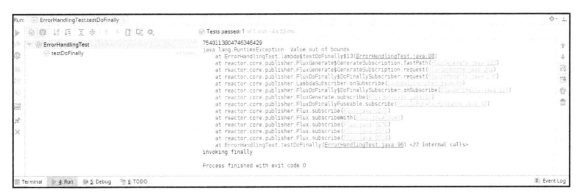

As an alternative to the `doFinally` hook, there is the `Flux.using` API. This API configures a resource mapped for a publisher. It also configures a callback lambda, which is invoked with the respective publisher resource upon stream closure. This is synonymous with the `try-with-resource` Java API:

```java
@Test
    public void testUsingMethod() {
        Flux<Long> fibonacciGenerator = Flux.generate(() -> Tuples.<Long,
                Long>of(0L, 1L), (state, sink) -> {
            if (state.getT1() < 0)
                sink.complete();
            else
                sink.next(state.getT1());

            return Tuples.of(state.getT2(), state.getT1() + state.getT2());
        });
        Closeable closable = () -> System.out.println("closing the
    stream");
        Flux.using(() -> closable, x -> fibonacciGenerator, e -> {
            try {
                e.close();
            } catch (Exception e1) {
```

```
                throw Exceptions.propagate(e1);
            }
        }).subscribe(System.out::println);
    }
```

The preceding code does the following:

1. It generates a `Flux<Long>` by invoking the `Using` API.
2. It maps a `closable` instance to an instance of `fibonacciGenerator`.
3. It invokes the `close` method upon stream completion. The `close` method can raise checked exceptions, so `Exceptions.propagate` is used to wrap the error.

Let's run the preceding test case and validate the output printed on the console, as follows:

Error recovery

In the preceding section, we determined how to configure an error callback. However, when performing error handling, we may encounter cases in which we want to continue execution with some alternative values. There are many use cases for such scenarios. For example, quote aggregating systems can have errors thrown while getting the latest tick value, but the aggregation must continue with the last value. In the following sections, we will cover each of the operators offered, in order to accomplish this.

The onErrorReturn operator

Reactor provides the `OnErrorReturn` operator to provide a fallback value in the event of an error. As a result of the fallback, the original error event is not propagated to the error callback. The event processing continues by using the event handler, as follows:

```
@Test
public void testErrorReturn() {
    Flux<Long> fibonacciGenerator = Flux.generate(() -> Tuples.<Long,
```

```
            Long>of(0L, 1L), (state, sink) -> {
        if (state.getT1() < 0)
            sink.error(new RuntimeException("Value out of bounds"));
        else
            sink.next(state.getT1());

        return Tuples.of(state.getT2(), state.getT1() + state.getT2());
    });
    fibonacciGenerator
            .onErrorReturn(0L)
            .subscribe(System.out::println);
}
```

In the preceding code, the following applies:

1. The `onErrorReturn` operator is used to provide 0 when an error is received by the subscriber
2. No error callback is configured in the subscriber API

Let's run our test case and validate the understanding of the preceding code:

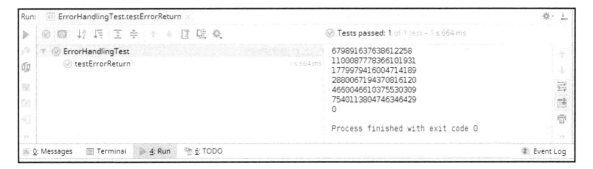

The `onErrorReturn` operator also provides exception-specific handling. This is an overloaded method that takes the exception class, as well as a fallback value. Reactor picks the first match it finds by validating whether or not the exception thrown is an instance of the exception configured. Consequently, we must configure the most specific exception matches first, and the most generic ones last. Now, let's write a test case to validate the exception handling, as follows:

```
    @Test
    public void testErrorReturn() {
        Flux<Long> fibonacciGenerator = Flux.generate(() -> Tuples.<Long,
                Long>of(0L, 1L), (state, sink) -> {
            if (state.getT1() < 0)
                sink.error(new IllegalStateException("Value out of
```

```
bounds"));
        // Removed for Brevity
      });
      fibonacciGenerator
            .onErrorReturn(RuntimeException.class,0L)
            .onErrorReturn(IllegalStateException.class,-1L)
            .subscribe(System.out::println);
    }
```

In the preceding code, we are now throwing `IllegalStateException`, instead of `RuntimeException`. `IllegalStateException` is a sub-type of `RuntimeException`. The subscriber is configured for both of these exceptions. It is important to note the order of the configuration here. `RuntimeException` has been configured first, with a default value of `0`, and the `IllegalStateException` with the value `-1`. Reactor will match the thrown exception against `RuntimeException`. Run the test case and validate the result here.

Finally, there is also an `onErrorReturn`, which matches the exception by validating it against the predicate provided. The configured predicate takes the exception thrown as input, and provides a Boolean result in return. Here, we also configure multiple predicates. Reactor will pick the first matching predicate and use its fallback value.

The onErrorResume operator

Similar to the `OnErrorReturn` operator, there is the `OnErrorResume` operator, which provides a fallback value stream instead of a single fallback value. In the event of an error, the fallback stream is returned. The original error event is not propagated to the error callback. The event processing continues by using the configured event handler, as follows:

```
@Test
public void testErrorResume() {
    Flux<Long> fibonacciGenerator = Flux.generate(() -> Tuples.<Long,
            Long>of(0L, 1L), (state, sink) -> {
      // Removed for Brevity
    });
    fibonacciGenerator
            .onErrorResume(x -> Flux.just(0L,-1L,-2L))
            .subscribe(System.out::println);
}
```

In the preceding code, the following applies:

1. The `onErrorResume` operator is used to provide back `Flux<Long>` when any error is received by the subscriber.
2. No error callback is configured in the subscriber API.

Let's run our test case and validate our understanding, as follows:

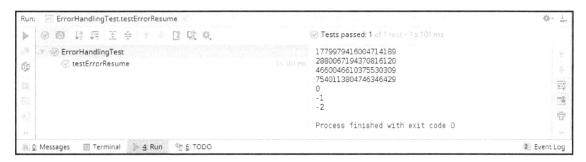

Similar to the lines of `onErrorReturn`, the `onErrorResume` operator is overloaded to provide specific, exception-based fallback values. Exceptions can be provided directly, or can be matched using a predicate. Reactor will pick the value that matches first.

The onErrorMap operator

Reactor's `onErrorMap` operator allows us to convert an exception of one type to another type. Unlike the previous two operators, the `onErrorMap` operator requires an error callback to be configured with the subscriber. If no handler is configured, the subscriber throws back an `ErrorCallbackNotImplemented` exception. The `onErrorMap` operator provides overloaded functions, similar to the previous operators, which can be used to match exceptions based on type or a provided predicate.

Now, let's build a simple test case to validate our understanding of the `onErrorMap` operator:

```
@Test
public void testErrorMap() {
    Flux<Long> fibonacciGenerator = Flux.generate(() -> Tuples.<Long,
            Long>of(0L, 1L), (state, sink) -> {
        // Removed for brevity
    });
    fibonacciGenerator
            .onErrorMap(x -> new IllegalStateException("Publisher threw
```

```
error", x))
                    .subscribe(System.out::println,System.out::println);
   }
```

In the preceding code, the following applies:

1. The `onErrorMap` operator is configured to throw `IllegalStateException` when any error is received by the subscriber.
2. The error callback was configured in the subscriber API.

Let's run it and confirm the output, as follows:

Timeout

As discussed in the preceding sections, generating a timely response is an important aspect of reactive systems. The requirement means that reactive systems must provide a deterministic response in a timely manner. However, all software systems are inherently unreliable. The underlying network itself is unreliable. All components can fail without providing a response. As a result, systems with streaming results can get stuck waiting for a response.

A way to address this unreliability is to adapt the fail-fast system design. This design dictates that a system makes some assumptions for normal operations, and it must fail as soon as these assumptions are broken. This leads to the early reporting of likely issues. In order to do this, we must assume a likely response time, the most common fail-fast metric. If the response is not received in this time, then the system must trigger the fallback/error response.

Reactor offers the `timeout()` operator to enable a response time check. The timeout fails when there is no response received in the specific time interval. Once the timeout expires, it triggers the error callback configured for the subscriber. Let's validate the operator by using the following code:

```java
@Test
public void testTimeout() throws  Exception{
    Flux<Long> fibonacciGenerator = Flux.generate(() -> Tuples.<Long,
            Long>of(0L, 1L), (state, sink) -> {
        if (state.getT1() < 0)
            throw new RuntimeException("Value out of bounds");
        else
            sink.next(state.getT1());

        return Tuples.of(state.getT2(), state.getT1() + state.getT2());
    });
    CountDownLatch countDownLatch = new CountDownLatch(1);
    fibonacciGenerator
            .delayElements(Duration.ofSeconds(1))
            .timeout(Duration.ofMillis(500))
            .subscribe(System.out::println, e -> {
                System.out.println(e);
                countDownLatch.countDown();
            });
    countDownLatch.await();
}
```

In the preceding code, the following applies:

1. The `delayElements` operator is responsible for slowing down each element by the configured time. In our case, it sends each element after a one second delay.

2. The `timeout()` operator is configured for an interval of 500 milliseconds. This operator will raise an error when it first discovers a delay of more than 500 milliseconds.

3. The `onError` callback is configured for the subscriber. We also added a `CountDownLatch`, as we want to hold the test execution until the error is received.

Let's run this and confirm the output, as follows:

The `timeout()` operator also offers to provide a fallback `Flux<>` value when the timeout is triggered. In this case, the fallback value does not throw a timeout error. Consequently, it does not trigger the configured error callbacks. Instead, the flow is executed as next events, as follows:

```
@Test
public void testTimeoutWithFallback() throws  Exception{
  // Removed for brevity
fibonacciGenerator
            .delayElements(Duration.ofSeconds(1))
            .timeout(Duration.ofMillis(500),Flux.just(-1L))
            .subscribe(e -> {
                System.out.println(e);
                countDownLatch.countDown();
            });
      countDownLatch.await();
}
```

In the preceding code, the following applies:

1. The `delayElements` operator is responsible for slowing down each element by the configured time. In our case, it sends each element after a one second delay.

2. The `timeout()` operator is configured for an interval of 500 milliseconds. This operator will raise an error when it first discovers a delay of more than 500 milliseconds. The operator also has a fallback Flux. The fallback value is returned once the timeout expires.

3. The `onNext` handler is configured to print the received value. We added a `CountDownLatch`, as we want to hold the test execution until the value is received.

4. There is no `onError` callback configured.

Let's run it and validate the output, as follows:

While we are discussing errors and timeouts, it is important to mention the `retry` operator. This operator allows us to re-subscribe to the published stream when an error is discovered. The retry can only be performed a fixed number of times. The re-subscribed events are handled as next events by the subscriber. If the stream completes normally, no next retry takes place. Error callback is only triggered when an error is thrown during the last retry cycle:

```
@Test
public void testRetry() throws  Exception{

  // Removed for brevity

    CountDownLatch countDownLatch = new CountDownLatch(1);
    fibonacciGenerator
            .retry(1)
            .subscribe(System.out::println, e -> {
                System.out.println("received :"+e);
                countDownLatch.countDown();
            },countDownLatch::countDown);
    countDownLatch.await();
}
```

In the preceding code, the following applies:

1. The `delayElements` operator is responsible for slowing down each element by the configured time. In our case, it sends each element after a one second delay.
2. The `timeout()` operator is configured for an interval of 500 milliseconds. The operator will raise an error when it first discovers a delay of more than 500 milliseconds. The operator also has a fallback Flux. The fallback value is returned once the timeout expires.
3. The `onNext` handler is configured to print the received value. We added a `CountDownLatch`, as we want to hold the test execution until the value is received.
4. No `onError` callback is configured.

Let's run it and validate the output, as follows:

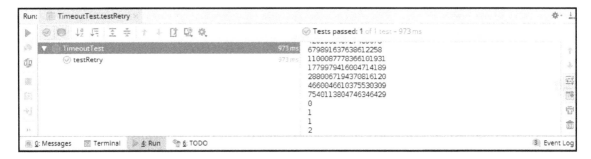

WebClient

In Chapter 6, *Dynamic Rendering*, we discussed using the Spring WebClient to make web calls in a non-blocking and asynchronous manner. The operators that we have discussed so far are applicable to Reactive Stream publishers and subscribers. WebClient also produces a Mono publisher of ServerResponse. So, how should we handle errors generated in WebClient, and generate a valid response? First, let's take a look at WebClient's default handling of server-side errors. To do this, we should first generate errors in our Fibonacci handler function, as follows:

```
@Bean
RouterFunction<ServerResponse> fibonacciEndpoint() {
    Flux<Long> fibonacciGenerator = Flux.generate(() -> Tuples.<Long,
            Long>of(0L, 1L), (state, sink) -> {
        throw new RuntimeException("Method unsupported");
    });
    RouterFunction<ServerResponse> fibonacciRoute =
            RouterFunctions.route(RequestPredicates.path("/fibonacci"),
                    request ->  ServerResponse.ok()
                            .body(fromPublisher(fibonacciGenerator,
Long.class)));

        return fibonacciRoute;
    }
```

In the preceding code, we modified our generator to raise a RuntimeException. The exception will be raised as soon as the server builds a response. This, in turn, sends the HTTP 500 status error back, with the exception message in the body:

Alternatively, we can raise an error using the `sink.error()` method. This method will take an exception instance and throw it back. It will also raise a 500 status code, with an `out of bound` error message, as follows:

```
@Bean
RouterFunction<ServerResponse> fibonacciEndpoint() {
    Flux<Long> fibonacciGenerator = Flux.generate(() -> Tuples.<Long,
            Long>of(0L, 1L), (state, sink) -> {
        if (state.getT1() < 0)
            sink.error(new RuntimeException("out of bound"));
        else
            sink.next(state.getT1());
        return Tuples.of(state.getT2(), state.getT1() + state.getT2());
    });

    // Rest removed for Brevity

    return fibonacciRoute;
}
```

We will invoke the preceding URL by using WebClient so as to understand its default behavior. Let's revisit the WebClient sample from Chapter 6, *Dynamic Rendering*:

```
Flux<Long> result = client.get()
        .uri("/fibonacci")
        .retrieve().bodyToFlux(Long.class)
        .limitRequest(10L);
result.subscribe( x-> System.out.println(x));
```

In the preceding code, the following applies:

1. We invoked the /fibonacci URL.
2. We converted the body, using the retrieve method.
3. We used the limit operator to select 10 results.
4. In the end, the results were printed to the console.

Note that there is no explicit error handler configured; run the code to see how it responds. The code does not generate any output or convert the body when it receives error status codes from the server. Alternatively, let's configure an error handler in the subscriber method and print the exception, as follows:

```
result.subscribe( x-> System.out.println(x), e-> e.printStackTrace);
```

Now, let's execute the WebClient code to determine the output:

```
org.springframework.web.reactive.function.client.WebClientResponseException
: ClientResponse has erroneous status code: 500 Internal Server Error
    at
org.springframework.web.reactive.function.client.DefaultWebClient$DefaultRe
sponseSpec.lambda$createResponseException$7(DefaultWebClient.java:464)
    at
reactor.core.publisher.FluxMap$MapSubscriber.onNext(FluxMap.java:100)
    at
 . . . . . . . . . . . . . .
```

Interestingly, this time around, we can see a WebClientResponseException, with the status code as an error message. If we look at the WebClientResponseException class, the exception allows us to get the response text, status code, and more. Typecasting the error and printing the response text would generate the following output:

```
{"timestamp":1533967357605,"path":"/fibonacci","status":500,"error":"Intern
al Server Error","message":"Unsupported Method"}
```

It is important to note the behavior of the WebClient API. Although the stream generated an error, we never saw the `ErrorCallbackNotImplemented` exception, unlike the behavior of Reactive Stream subscribers without a configured error handler.

WebClient works well with the `onError` operators that were discussed in the previous sections. We can configure either `onErrorReturn` or `onErrorResume` operators. This would provide fallback values, which are returned in the case of an error, as follows:

```
Flux<Long> result = client.get()
        .uri("/fibonacci")
        .retrieve()
        .bodyToFlux(Long.class)
        .onErrorResume( x -> Flux.just(-1L, -2L))
        .limitRequest(10L);
result.subscribe( x-> System.out.println(x));
```

Now, execute the preceding code and confirm the fallback values in the output.

Here, the WebClient that retrieves an API also offers an `onStatus` method to configure response handling. The `onStatus` method takes exception mapping and invokes it for the configured HTTP status codes. In our preceding sample, let's try to throw a `RuntimeException` for a 500 server response:

```
Flux<Long> result = client.get()
        .uri("/fibonacci")
        .retrieve()
        .onStatus(HttpStatus::isError, x -> Mono.error(new
         RuntimeException("Invalid Response ")))
        .bodyToFlux(Long.class)
        .limitRequest(10L);
```

In the preceding code, the following applies:

- `RuntimeException` is raised as `Mono.error`.
- The Mono is configured for all HTTP error status codes (4XX, 5XX).

When the preceding code is executed, a `RuntimeException` is thrown. However, the exception leads to an `ErrorCallbackNotImplemented` exception, unlike the previous behavior, where `WebClientResponseException` did not ask for an exception handler:

```
reactor.core.Exceptions$ErrorCallbackNotImplemented:
java.lang.RuntimeException: Invalid Response
Caused by: java.lang.RuntimeException: Invalid Response
```

Now, we can configure exception mapping or a fallback value provider to recover from the thrown exception.

Summary

In this chapter, we looked at the various ways to add resilience to our application. First, we covered possible error scenarios involving the producer and the subscriber. Next, we looked at how Reactor performs error handling under each of those conditions. This enabled us to configure the required error handling in Reactor, by using the various operations that are offered. Reactor allows us to configure fallback values for the thrown exceptions by using onErrorReturn and onErrorResume operators. We also configured timeouts and retry machines, using the available operators, in order to generate timely responses. Finally, we configured error handling in WebClient. In a nutshell, we explored the possible ways to configure error handlers in Reactor.

Questions

1. How is an error handled in Reactor?
2. Which operators allow us to configure error handling?
3. What is the difference between onErrorResume and onErrorReturn?
4. How can we generate a timely response for a Reactive Stream?
5. How does the retry operator behave?

9
Execution Control

Throughout this book, we have been working with Reactor operators. This has included performing various tasks, such as filtering, transforming, and collecting. Most operators do not create additional threads and just work on the main thread. However, we can configure multithreading and concurrency in Reactor by using a set of schedulers.

We will cover the following topics in this chapter:

- Schedulers
- Parallel processing
- Broadcasting

Technical requirements

- Java Standard Edition, JDK 8 or above
- IntelliJ IDEA IDE, 2018.1 or above

The GitHub link for this chapter is `https://github.com/PacktPublishing/Hands-On-Reactive-Programming-with-Reactor/tree/master/Chapter09`.

Scheduler

Reactor executes all operations using one of the schedulers. A Reactor scheduler does not belong to the `java.util.concurrent` API. The Java concurrent API is quite low-level, where we can initiate and control task execution. On the other hand, all tasks in a Reactor chain are executed by the Reactor engine. Consequently, we do not need a low-level API to manage task execution. Instead, Reactor offers a declarative model, which we can use to configure a `Scheduler` and alter the behavior of the chain execution.

Before we start to configure Reactor, let's first determine the default execution model. By default, Reactor is mostly single-threaded. The publisher and subscriber do not create additional threads for their execution. All life cycle hooks, and most operators, perform single-threaded execution. Before we jump ahead, let's build some code to validate this, as follows:

```
@Test
public void testReactorThread() throws Exception{
    Flux<Long> fibonacciGenerator = Flux.generate(() -> Tuples.<Long,
            Long>of(0L, 1L), (state, sink) -> {
        if (state.getT1() < 0)
            sink.complete();
        else
            sink.next(state.getT1());
        print("Generating next of "+ state.getT2());
        return Tuples.of(state.getT2(), state.getT1() + state.getT2());
    });
    fibonacciGenerator
            .filter(x -> {
                print("Executing Filter");
                return x < 100;
            })
            .doOnNext(x -> print("Next value is  "+x))
            .doFinally(x -> print("Closing "))
            .subscribe(x -> print("Sub received : "+x));
}

static void print(String text){
    System.out.println("["+Thread.currentThread().getName()+"] "+text);
}
```

In the preceding code, the following applies:

1. We built a simple Fibonacci chain, using the `filter` operator and life cycle hooks.
2. Each operation prints to a console using the `print` function.
3. The `print` function prints the current thread name, along with the text.

The following screenshot shows a simple debugging code snippet, which allows us to see how Reactor does stream execution. Let's run this and see how it works:

In the preceding screenshot, we can see that all of the text is prefixed with [main].
Consequently, all operations are executed on the main thread, and no additional threads
are used by Reactor. This output validates the idea that Reactor is single-threaded, by
default. Due to the single-threaded execution, we did not pause the test execution
using `Thread.sleep` or `latch.wait`.

However, the preceding concept is only partially true; Reactor operators do alter the
behavior of chain execution. Previously, we used `latch` and `Thread.sleep` in our test
cases, for the delay and timeout operator. Let's add the operator to our test case and
analyze the output, as follows:

```
@Test
    public void testReactorDelayThread() throws Exception{
        // Removed for brevity
        fibonacciGenerator
                .filter(x -> {
                    print("Executing Filter");
                    return x < 100;
                }).delayElements(Duration.ZERO)
                .doOnNext(x -> print("Next value is  "+x))
                .doFinally(x -> print("Closing "))
                .subscribe(x -> print("Sub received : "+x));
        Thread.sleep(500);
    }
```

In the preceding code, the following applies:

1. We added the `delayElements` operator to our chain, after the `filter` operator.
2. The test now terminates quickly, so we need to add `Thread.sleep` to pause the
   execution of the main thread. The pause ensures that the complete chain is
   executed.

Let's run this and analyze the output, as follows:

We can deduce the following by looking at the preceding output:

- The publisher does not create a thread; it executes in the main thread.
- The `filter` operation does not create a thread; it executes in the main thread.
- The `delayElements` operations add a thread pool of two threads, denoted by `parallel-1` and `parallel-2`.
- The rest of the chain now executes in the thread pool, rather than the main thread.

Now that you have gained some understanding of the threading model of Reactor, let's discuss the ways in which we can configure it.

Reactor schedulers

As discussed in the previous section, Reactor operators configure reactive chain execution behavior. However, the behavior can be altered by using a different scheduler. Most of the operators have overloaded methods, which take a scheduler as an argument. In this section, we will look at the various schedulers available in Reactor. Reactor also provides a `schedulers` utility class, to build instances of the available implementations.

The immediate scheduler

The `Schedulers.immediate` scheduler executes work on the currently executing thread. All tasks are executed on the caller thread, and no task is performed in parallel. This is the default execution model for most Reactor tasks. Consider the following code:

```
@Test
  public void testImmediateSchedular() throws Exception{

        // Removed for Brevity
```

```
fibonacciGenerator
        .delayElements(Duration.ofNanos(10),Schedulers.immediate())
        .doOnNext(x -> print("Next value is  "+x))
        .doFinally(x -> print("Closing "))
    .subscribe(x -> print("Sub received : "+x));
Thread.sleep(500);
}
```

In the preceding code, the following has occurred:

1. We added the `delayElements` operator to our chain.
2. The test tries to schedule the delay on the main thread.

We can execute the code, but the task will fail, because the main thread lacks the time-based scheduling capability. The following screenshot shows this:

The single scheduler

The `Schedulers.single` scheduler executes work on a single-worker thread pool. Since this is a single worker, all tasks are executed one by one, and no task is performed in a concurrent manner. The scheduler is quite useful for isolating the execution of non-threadsafe operations to a single thread. Consider the following code:

```
@Test
  public void testSingleScheduler() throws Exception{

    // Removed for Brevity

    fibonacciGenerator
            .delayElements(Duration.ofNanos(10),Schedulers.single())
            .doOnNext(x -> print("Next value is  "+x))
            .doFinally(x -> print("Closing "))
        .subscribe(x -> print("Sub received : "+x));
    Thread.sleep(500);
}
```

In the preceding code, the following has occurred:

1. We added the `delayElements` operator to our chain.
2. The test tries to schedule the delay on a single thread, and not on the main thread of test execution.

From the output, we can validate that all of the tasks in the chain are executed on a `single-1` thread. Consider the following screenshot:

Here, the `single` scheduler is meant to execute non-blocking, computation-intensive operations. This can be treated as an event loop, executing non-blocking tasks in its queue. If we invoke any reactive blocking APIs, the scheduler throws back the following error:

```
@Test
    public void testSingleSchedulerBlockingOps() throws Exception{
        // Removed for Brevity
        fibonacciGenerator
                .filter(x -> {
                    print("Executing Filter");
                    return x < 100;
                }).delayElements(Duration.ZERO,Schedulers.single())
                .window(10)
                .doOnNext(x -> print("Next value is  "+x))
                .doFinally(x -> print("Closing "+x))
                .subscribe(x -> print("Sub received : "+x.blockFirst()));
        Thread.sleep(500);
    }
```

In addition to the chain discussed previously, the following has occurred in the preceding code:

1. We invoked the `window` operator to generate batches of 10 elements each.
2. The subscriber invoked the `blockFirst` API to get back the first element.

Executing the preceding code leads to the following exception:

The parallel scheduler

The `Schedulers.parallel` scheduler executes work on a multiple-worker thread pool. It creates workers based on the number of available processors. This is the default scheduler used in various Reactor operators. Consider the following code:

```
@Test
    public void testParalleScheduler() throws Exception{

        // Removed for Brevity

        fibonacciGenerator
                .delayElements(Duration.ofNanos(10),Schedulers.parallel())
                .doOnNext(x -> print("Next value is  "+x))
                .doFinally(x -> print("Closing "))
            .subscribe(x -> print("Sub received : "+x));
        Thread.sleep(500);
    }
```

From the output, we can validate that all of the tasks in the chain are executed on `paralle-1` and `parallel-2` threads. Go through the following screenshot:

Similar to the `single` scheduler, the `parallel` scheduler is aimed at executing non-blocking tasks. If an operation invokes any of the reactive blocking APIs, the scheduler will throw back the following exception:

```
Caused by: java.lang.IllegalStateException:
block()/blockFirst()/blockLast() are blocking, which is not supported in
thread parallel-1
    at
reactor.core.publisher.BlockingSingleSubscriber.blockingGet(BlockingSingleS
ubscriber.java:77)
    at reactor.core.publisher.Flux.blockFirst(Flux.java:2013)
    at
SchedulerTest.lambda$testSingleSchedulerBlockingOps$27(SchedulerTest.java:1
16)
```

The elastic scheduler

The `Schedulers.elastic` scheduler executes work on a multiple-worker thread pool. Each of the executed workers can execute long-lived tasks that ask for a blocking operation. Each worker is returned to the pool when the task finishes. There is also an idle time associated with the worker, after which the worked is disposed. The scheduler tries to consume an existing idle worker, but if there aren't any, the scheduler dynamically generates one and schedules the task on it. The following code shows this:

```
@Test
    public void testElasticSchedular() throws Exception{

        // Removed for Brevity

        fibonacciGenerator
                .filter(x -> {
                    print("Executing Filter");
                    return x < 100;
                }).delayElements(Duration.ZERO,Schedulers.elastic())
                .window(10)
                .doOnNext(x -> print("Next value is  "+ x))
                .doFinally(x -> print("Closing "+x))
                .subscribe(x -> print("Sub received : "+x.blockFirst()));
        Thread.sleep(500);
    }
```

Unlike the previous worker, a blocking reactive call executes on an elastic scheduler successfully. Consider the following screenshot:

The ExecutorService scheduler

The `Schedulers.fromExecutor` enables us to build a scheduler over the Java `ExecutorService`. The scheduler does not own thread generation, but instead, it is controlled by the underlying `ExecutorService`. The scheduler should not be favored over other schedulers, as the life cycle of the `ExecutorService` must be managed by the developer. Consider the following code:

```
@Test
    public void testExecutorScheduler() throws Exception{
        // Removed for Brevity

        ExecutorService executor = Executors.newSingleThreadExecutor();
        fibonacciGenerator
                .filter(x -> {
                    print("Executing Filter");
                    return x < 100;
}).delayElements(Duration.ZERO,Schedulers.fromExecutor(executor))
                .doOnNext(x -> print("Next value is  "+ x))
                .doFinally(x -> print("Closing "+executor.isShutdown()))
                .subscribe(x -> print("Sub received : "+x));
        Thread.sleep(5000);
        print("Is shutdown ? "+executor.isShutdown());
    }
```

In the following output, we can validate that the service is still running after the execution of our reactive chain:

Parallel processing

Reactor publishers and subscribers do not create threads. However, as seen in the previous section, there are operators that can alter this behavior. In the last section, we saw that the `delay` operator moved the execution of the Reactor chain from the main thread to the scheduler thread. However, we do not need delay/timeout operators for the purpose of switching execution. Reactor offers the `publishOn` and `subscribeOn` operators for the purpose of switching the chain execution. Both of these operators change the execution context of the reactive chain to the configured scheduler.

PublishOn operator

The `publishOn` operator intercepts events from a publisher at a configured point in the execution chain, and sends them to a different scheduler for the rest of the chain. As a result, the operator changes the threading context of the downstream reactive chain. It is important to note that the operator only influences the downstream event chain. It does not alter the upstream chain, and leaves the upstream execution to the default execution model. The following code shows this:

```
@Test
public void testReactorPublishOn() throws Exception{
    Flux<Long> fibonacciGenerator = Flux.generate(() -> Tuples.<Long,
            Long>of(0L, 1L), (state, sink) -> {
        if (state.getT1() < 0)
            sink.complete();
        else
            sink.next(state.getT1());
        print("Generating next of "+ state.getT2());
        return Tuples.of(state.getT2(), state.getT1() + state.getT2());
    });
```

```
fibonacciGenerator
        .publishOn(Schedulers.single())
        .filter(x -> {
            print("Executing Filter");
            return x < 100;
        })
        .doOnNext(x -> print("Next value is   "+x))
        .doFinally(x -> print("Closing "))
        .subscribe(x -> print("Sub received : "+x));
    Thread.sleep(500);
}
```

In the preceding code, the following applies:

1. We configured the `publishOn` operator before the `filter` operator. This should leave the generation on the main thread, and execute the rest of the chain on the scheduler.
2. We configured the `single` scheduler for the chain execution.
3. Since we are not executing the chain on the main thread, we have to pause the test execution for some time. This is accomplished by using `Thread.sleep`.

Let's execute the test case and determine the output. The publisher generates events on the `main` thread, which are then passed over to a `single-1` thread, as shown in the following screenshot:

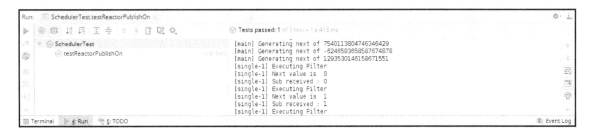

SubscribeOn operator

The `subscribeOn` operator intercepts events from a publisher in the execution chain and sends them to a different scheduler for the complete chain. It is important to note that the operator changes the execution context for the complete chain, unlike the `publishOn` operator, which only alters the execution of a downstream chain:

```
@Test
    public void testReactorSubscribeOn() throws Exception{
```

```
Flux<Long> fibonacciGenerator = Flux.generate(() -> Tuples.<Long,
        Long>of(0L, 1L), (state, sink) -> {
    if (state.getT1() < 0)
        sink.complete();
    else
        sink.next(state.getT1());
    print("Generating next of "+ state.getT2());
    return Tuples.of(state.getT2(), state.getT1() + state.getT2());
});
fibonacciGenerator
        .filter(x -> {
            print("Executing Filter");
            return x < 100;
        })
        .doOnNext(x -> print("Next value is  "+x))
        .doFinally(x -> print("Closing "))
        .subscribeOn(Schedulers.single())
        .subscribe(x -> print("Sub received : "+x));
Thread.sleep(500);
}
```

In the preceding code, we did the following:

1. Configured the `subscribeOn` operator, prior to subscribing.
2. Configured the `single` scheduler for the chain execution.
3. Since we are not executing the chain on the main thread, we have to pause the test execution for some time. This is accomplished by using `Thread.sleep`.

Let's execute the test case and validate the output. All of the events are generated on the single thread configured by the `subscribeOn` operator:

We have the `subscribeOn` and `publishOn` operators in the same chain. The `subscribeOn` operator will execute the complete reactive chain on the configured scheduler. However, the `publishOn` operator will change the downstream chain to the specified scheduler. It leaves back the upstream chain on the scheduler configured by the `subscribeOn` scheduler:

```
@Test
    public void testReactorComposite() throws Exception{
        // Removed for Brevity
        fibonacciGenerator
                .publishOn(Schedulers.parallel())
                .filter(x -> {
                    print("Executing Filter");
                    return x < 100;
                })
                .doOnNext(x -> print("Next value is  "+x))
                .doFinally(x -> print("Closing "))
                .subscribeOn(Schedulers.single())
                .subscribe(x -> print("Sub received : "+x));
        Thread.sleep(500);
    }
```

The preceding code will generate events on a `single-1` scheduler, configured by the `subscribeOn` operator. The rest of the chain is executed on a parallel scheduler, configured by the `publishOn` operator.

The following is the output after running the preceding code:

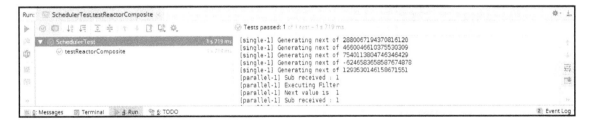

ParallelFlux

Reactor offers `ParallelFlux`, which is capable of splitting an existing stream into multiple streams in a round-robin manner. `ParallelFlux` is created from an existing `Flux`, using the `parallel` operator. By default, this splits the stream into the total number of CPU cores that are available. `ParallelFlux` only divides the stream, and does not change the execution model. Instead, it executes the streams on the default thread—the main thread. The divided stream can be configured for parallel processing by using the `runOn` operator. Similar to the `publishOn` operator, the `runOn` takes a scheduler and executes the downstream on the specified scheduler.

It is important to note that `ParallelFlux` does not offer the `doFinally` life cycle hook. It can be converted back to a `Flux` by using the `sequential` operator, which can then be configured by using the `doFinally` hook:

```
@Test
    public void testParalleFlux() throws Exception{
       // Removed for Brevity

        fibonacciGenerator
                .parallel()
                .runOn(Schedulers.parallel())
                .filter(x -> {
                    print("Executing Filter");
                    return x < 100;
                })
                .doOnNext(x -> print("Next value is   "+x))
                .sequential()
                .doFinally(x -> print("Closing "))
                .subscribeOn(Schedulers.single())
                .subscribe(x -> print("Sub received : "+x));
        Thread.sleep(500);
    }
```

In the preceding code, the following applies:

1. The `parallel` operator is configured to generate `ParallelFlux` from `fibonacciGenerator`.
2. The `runOn` operator is used to configure `ParallelFlux` on the parallel scheduler.
3. The `sequential` operator is used to convert `ParallelFlux` to Flux.
4. `doFinally` is configured on the `sequential` Flux.
5. `subscribeOn` is configured to execute Flux generation on a single thread.

Let's run the code and validate the output, as follows:

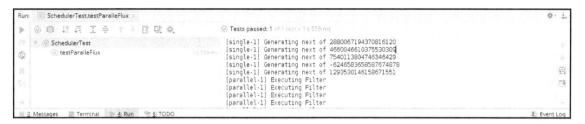

So far, we have discussed how to perform stream operations in parallel. In the next section, we will deliver events to all subscribers simultaneously, and then configure parallel processing for all of them.

Broadcasting

In networking, **broadcasting** is defined as simultaneous event publishing to multiple receivers. In terms of Reactive Streams, this means simultaneous event publishing to multiple subscribers. Until now, we have subscribed to cold publishers, where each subscription generates a new series of events. We have even subscribed to hot publishers, where the publisher keeps pushing events without waiting for a subscriber. Each subscriber gets the same event as soon as it is generated. A hot publisher may look like a broadcasting event, but there is a key difference with regard to the start of the event generation stream. Reactor allows us to create a `ConnecatableFlux`, capable of waiting for *n* subscribers before starting event generation. It then keeps publishing each event to all of its subscribers.

The replay operator

Reactor provides the `replay` operator to convert a Flux to a `ConnectableFlux`. The resulting `ConnectableFlux` keeps buffering events published to the first subscriber. The buffer can be configured to keep the last *n* entries, or it can be configured to be based on the time duration. Only the buffered events are replayed back to the subscribers.

Refer to the following diagram:

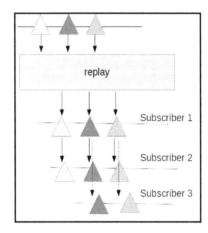

A `ConnectableFlux` must be subscribed by *n* subscribers before it starts to publish events. `ConnectableFlux` provides the following operators to manage subscribers:

- **Connect**: The `connect` operator must be invoked after enough subscriptions have been made. We must manage the subscription count ourselves. Subscription cancellation must also be tracked by developers.
- **Auto-Connect**: The `autoConnect` operator configures a subscription count. This keeps track of subscriptions made to the publisher dynamically. It is best to use the `autoConnect` operator, and leave the subscription management to Reactor.

Let's take a look at the following code:

```
@Test
public void testReplayBroadcast() throws Exception{
    // Removed for Brevity
    Flux<Long> broadcastGenerator=fibonacciGenerator.doFinally(x -> {
        System.out.println("Closing ");
    }).replay().autoConnect(2);


    fibonacciGenerator.subscribe(x -> System.out.println("[Fib] 1st :
"+x));
    fibonacciGenerator.subscribe(x -> System.out.println("[Fib] 2nd :
"+x));

    broadcastGenerator.subscribe(x -> System.out.println("1st : "+x));
    broadcastGenerator.subscribe(x -> System.out.println("2nd : "+x));
}
```

In the preceding code, you can see the following:

1. The `broadcastGenerator` is generated from `fibonacciGenerator`, using the `replay` operator.
2. The `broadcastGenerator` waits for two subscribers before starting event publishing.
3. `fibonacciGenerator` is subscribed twice.
4. `broadcastGenerator` is also subscribed twice.

In the preceding code, we have subscribed twice, to both the `fibonacciGenerator` and `broadcastGenerator` publishers. Let's run the test case and validate the output, as follows:

In the preceding screenshot (output), we can see that the `fibonacciGenerator` publisher is called every time the next value is requested by the respective publisher. However, the `broadcastGenerator` publisher is invoked once, and the same value is published to both subscribers before generating the next value.

The `connect` and `autoConnect` operators, discussed in the preceding section, only keep track of subscription events. These start to process events when the configured count is reached. They keep publishing them until the publisher sends a terminating event. These operators do not keep track of a subscriber cancelling the subscription; once event generation has started, it keeps generating events, even when the subscribers have cancelled their subscription.

Reactor provides a `refCount` operator for the previously discussed situation. The `refCount` operator also keeps track of the subscription. It stops generating new events if all subscribers have cancelled their subscription, as follows:

```
@Test
    public void testBroadcastWithCancel() throws Exception{
        // removed for brevity
```

```
        fibonacciGenerator=fibonacciGenerator.doFinally(x ->
System.out.println("Closing "))
        .replay().autoConnect(2);

    fibonacciGenerator.subscribe(new BaseSubscriber<Long>() {
        @Override
        protected void hookOnSubscribe(Subscription subscription) {
            request(1);
        }

        @Override
        protected void hookOnNext(Long value) {
            System.out.println("1st: "+value);
            cancel();
        }
    });

    fibonacciGenerator.subscribe(new BaseSubscriber<Long>() {
        @Override
        protected void hookOnNext(Long value) {
            System.out.println("2nd : "+value);
            cancel();
        }
    });
    Thread.sleep(500);

}
```

In the preceding code, the following applies:

- The `fibonacciGenerator` is configured for two subscribers, before starting event publishing.
- Each subscriber requests one event.
- Each subscriber cancels its subscription while processing the generated event.

Let's run the following test case to get the output, as follows:

```
Run:    BroadcastTest.testBroadcastWithCancel

    BroadcastTest                                  Tests passed: 1 of 1 test - 5 s 308 ms
        testBroadcastWithCancel         5 s 308 ms  generating next of 2880067194370816120
                                                    generating next of 4660046610375530309
                                                    generating next of 7540113804746346429
                                                    generating next of -6246583658587674878
                                                    Closing
                                                    generating next of 1293530146158671551

                                                    Process finished with exit code 0
```

In the preceding output, we can see that the complete Fibonacci series is generated before the stream is closed. The subscribers did not ask for more than one event. Now, let's replace `autoConnect` with `refCount`, and compare the output:

In the preceding output, you can see that the stream is closed as soon as all subscribers have cancelled their subscription. Now, if new subscribers arrive at `ConnectedFlux`, the series is generated from the first event.

The publish operator

Reactor provides the `publish` operator to generate a `ConnectedFlux`. Unlike the `replay` operator, which buffers events received by the first subscriber, the `publish` operator gets events from the source stream. The operator keeps track of the demands raised by its subscribers. If any subscriber does not raise a demand, it pauses the event generation until a new demand is raised by all of its subscribers. Consider the following diagram:

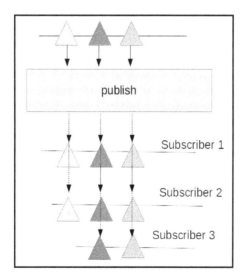

Just like the `replay` operator, the `ConnectedFlux` generated by the publisher also needs subscriber management. Here, we can configure this by using any of the following three options—`connect`, `autoConnect`, or `refCount`:

```java
@Test
    public void testPublishBroadcast() throws Exception{
        Flux<Long> fibonacciGenerator = Flux.generate(() -> Tuples.<Long,
                Long>of(0L, 1L), (state, sink) -> {
            if (state.getT1() < 0)
                sink.complete();
            else
                sink.next(state.getT1());
            System.out.println("generating next of "+ state.getT2());

            return Tuples.of(state.getT2(), state.getT1() + state.getT2());
        });
        fibonacciGenerator=fibonacciGenerator.doFinally(x -> {
            System.out.println("Closing ");
        }).publish().autoConnect(2);

        fibonacciGenerator.subscribe(new BaseSubscriber<Long>() {
            @Override
            protected void hookOnSubscribe(Subscription subscription) {
                request(1);
            }

            @Override
            protected void hookOnNext(Long value) {
                System.out.println("1st: "+value);
            }
        });

        fibonacciGenerator.subscribe(x -> System.out.println("2nd : "+x));
        Thread.sleep(500);

    }
```

In the preceding code, the following applies:

1. The `fibonacciGenerator` is configured for two subscribers, before starting event publishing.
2. The first subscriber requests only one event.
3. The second subscriber does not put a constraint on the event count.

Let's run the test case to analyze the output, as follows:

In the preceding output, you can see that only the first event is generated. There is no closing event either, because the stream was waiting for the next event request from subscriber one. Consequently, the stream did not terminate. The test finished after waiting for 500 ms.

Summary

In this chapter, we explored Reactor execution models. We discovered that publisher and subscriber Reactive Streams are concurrency agnostic. Most of the operators in Reactor are also concurrency agnostic. Some operators, such as delayElements and timeout, do alter the concurrency behavior of a stream's execution. Reactor provides various schedulers, which can be used to control the execution behavior of the stream. We found out that these schedulers can be configured for various operators, such as publishOn and subscribeOn. Next, we discussed ParallelFlux, which can be configured, along with the available schedulers, to perform parallel processing. Finally, we discussed event broadcasting by using ConnectedFlux. Reactor presents replay and publishOn operators, to generate a ConnectedFlux from an existing Flux.

Questions

1. What are the different types of schedulers that are available in Reactor?
2. What scheduler should be used for blocking operations?
3. What scheduler should be used for computation-intensive operations?
4. How are PublishOn and SubscriberOn different from each other?
5. What is the limitation of ParallelFlux?
6. Which operators are available for generating a ConnectedFlux?

10
Testing and Debugging

Throughout this book, we have covered Reactor in great detail, working with its various operators and building examples using them. However, writing code is only half of the job. All production code must also be verified with adequate unit tests. These tests not only validate our code, but they also enable us to make changes faster. If we refactor code, the tests ensure that our change has not broken any existing functionality. In this chapter, we will cover the testing support offered by Reactor. Testing business code will catch most of the issues, but the code will fail in production. In such scenarios, the code needs to be debugged in order to find the root cause of the failure. In this chapter, we will also cover some basic techniques to debug Reactor pipelines.

In this final chapter, we will learn how to:

- Test Reactor pipelines
- Debug Reactor streams

Technical requirements

- Java Standard Edition, JDK 8 or above
- IntelliJ IDEA IDE 2018.1 or above

The GitHub link for this chapter is `https://github.com/PacktPublishing/Hands-On-Reactive-Programming-with-Reactor/tree/master/Chapter10`.

Testing Reactor pipelines

Unit testing Reactor pipelines is quite hard. This is because Reactor declares behaviors rather than states that can be validated. Fortunately, Reactor comes with utility classes that can assist in unit testing. The testing utilities are bundled in the `reactor-test` component. `reactor-test` provides us with the following three components:

- `StepVerifier`: Allows us to validate a pipeline configuration and operators
- `TestPublisher`: Allows us to produce test data to enable testing operators
- `PublisherProbe`: Enables us to validate an existing publisher

Before we proceed, let's first add `reactor-test` to our `build.gradle`. We do not need to specify the version of this as that is defined by the `org.springframework.boot` plugin:

```
plugins {
    id "io.spring.dependency-management" version "1.0.1.RELEASE"
    id "org.springframework.boot" version "2.0.3.RELEASE"
    id "java"
}

// Removed for brevity

dependencies {
        compile 'org.springframework.boot:spring-boot-starter-webflux'
        compile 'org.springframework:spring-context-support'
        compile group: 'org.freemarker', name: 'freemarker', version:
'2.3.28'
        testCompile group: 'junit', name: 'junit', version: '4.12'
        testCompile 'io.projectreactor:reactor-test'
}
```

Now, let's run `./gradlew clean deploy`. After doing this, we should find that we have a successful build.

StepVerifier

Before now, we have tested final outcomes for each Reactive Stream as the complete pipeline was created in the test case. This approach is not a good unit test as it does not validate the components in isolation. In Reactor, pipelines are declared in code. These pipelines are then lazily instantiated and verified. Since a complete pipeline is instantiated, it is quite difficult to unit test components in isolation. For unit testing, we must have the ability to stub the components of a pipeline, leaving behind the component being tested. But in this case, how can we validate an existing pipeline for the sequence of operations? Reactor provides the `StepVerifier` component to validate the required operations in isolation. This API not only defines stubs, but also provides assertions to validate each step. In this section, we will work with various examples of validating different Reactor scenarios. Let's start with the simplest use case where, given a publisher, we may want to assert the `next` and `completion` events published by it:

```
@Test
public void testExpectation() throws Exception {
    Flux<Long> fibonacciGenerator = Flux.generate(() -> Tuples.<Long,
            Long>of(0L, 1L), (state, sink) -> {
        if (state.getT1() < 0)
            sink.complete();
        else
            sink.next(state.getT1());
        System.out.println("generating next of " + state.getT1());

        return Tuples.of(state.getT2(), state.getT1() + state.getT2());
    });
    StepVerifier.create(fibonacciGenerator.take(10))
            .expectNext(0L, 1L, 1L)
            .expectNextCount(7)
            .expectComplete()
            .verify();
}
```

In the preceding code, we are validating Fibonacci series operations as follows:

- We have configured the `take` operator to consume only 10 events.
- Next, we used the `StepVerifier.Create` API to build an instance of a verfier.
- The `expectNext` API is used to validate published values in the published order. This takes a single value or an array of values; we are validating the 0, 1, and 1 values.

- `expectNextCount` is used to validate the number of published values. Since we validate three values, we are left with seven more.
- The `expectComplete` API is used to validate a completion event.
- At the end, the `verify` API is used to validate the behavior.

Now, let's run the test case. When doing this, we should see a green bar:

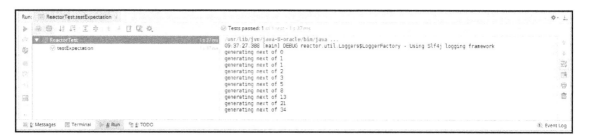

If `expectNext` does not match the published values, the test fails with `java.lang.AssertionError` and detailed error text. If the published count differs, then it does not fail with `expectNextCount`, but `expectComplete`. In all assertion failures, `StepVerifier` throws a `java.lang.AssertionError` with the following detailed message:

```
java.lang.AssertionError: expectation "expectComplete" failed (expected:
onComplete(); actual: onNext(34))
    at
reactor.test.DefaultStepVerifierBuilder.failPrefix(DefaultStepVerifierBuild
er.java:2235)
    at
reactor.test.DefaultStepVerifierBuilder.fail(DefaultStepVerifierBuilder.jav
a:2231)
    at
reactor.test.DefaultStepVerifierBuilder.lambda$expectComplete$4(DefaultStep
VerifierBuilder.java:245)
```

In the following sections, we will discuss the most commonly used methods available in `StepVerfier`.

expectError

As discussed throughout this book, a Reactive Stream terminates with a completion or error event. Similarly to `expectComplete`, for a completion event, there is the `expectError` API to validate error events. The `expectError` API offers the following convenient methods to validate an error message or the exception class:

Error name	Description
`expectError()`	The API only validates the occurrence of an error event. It does not validate any details about the error.
`expectError(exceptionClass)`	The API validates the underlying exception class wrapped in the error event.
`expectErrorMessage(errorMessage)`	The API validates the underlying exception message wrapped in the error event.
`expectError(Predicate)`	The API validates the underlying exception using the configured predicate.

In all preceding cases, `StepVerifier` asserts the exception wrapped in the error event. If the error does not match, an `assertionError` is thrown by `StepVerifier`. `StepVerifier` also provides an `expectErrorSatisfies` API, which can be used to configure customs assertions. This API takes a `Consumer` to assert an exception underlying the error event:

```
@Test
    public void testErrorExpectation() throws Exception {
        Flux<Long> fibonacciGenerator = Flux.generate(() -> Tuples.<Long,
                Long>of(0L, 1L), (state, sink) -> {
            if (state.getT1() > 30)
                sink.error(new IllegalStateException("Value out of
bound"));

            // Removed for brevity
        });
        StepVerifier.create(fibonacciGenerator.take(10))
                .expectNextCount(9)
                .expectErroSatisfies(x -> {
                    assert(x instanceof IllegalStateException);
                })
                .verify();
    }
```

In the preceding code, we are throwing an exception when the value goes above `30`. `expectErrorSatisfies` asserts that the exception thrown is an `IllegalStateException` type. Let's execute the preceding test case to get a green bar for a successful test case. This is shown with the following screenshot:

expectNext

Reactor provides multiple methods to assert next values. In the preceding code, we matched values using the `expectNext()` overloaded operator. This operator is offered in the following variants:

Operator	Description
`expectNext(value1,value2..value6)`	This method verifies the published values against the supplied values. The values must be matched in the order specified.
`expectNext(value[])`	This method verifies the published values against the supplied value array. All values must be matched in the order specified.
`expectNextSequence(Iterator)`	This method verifies the published values against values from the configured iterator. All values must be matched in the order specified.
`expectNextCount(count)`	This method matches the number of values published.
`expectNextMatches(predicate)`	This method validates whether or not the next values satisfy the configured predicate.

All of the preceding methods validate the next published value against a matching expectation. This is good for small datasets, but when we are publishing large ranges such as the Fibonacci series, we cannot match all values. Sometimes, we are just interested in consuming all (or some) next values. This can be accomplished by using the thenConsumeWhile API. The methods take a predicate and then consume all sequenced values matching the predicate. Once the first value mismatches, the test case tries to validate the following configured expectation:

```
@Test
public void testConsumeWith() throws Exception {
    Flux<Long> fibonacciGenerator = Flux.generate(() -> Tuples.<Long,
            Long>of(0L, 1L), (state, sink) -> {
        if (state.getT1() < 0)
            sink.complete();
        else
            sink.next(state.getT1());
        System.out.println("generating next of " + state.getT2());

        return Tuples.of(state.getT2(), state.getT1() + state.getT2());
    });

    StepVerifier.create(fibonacciGenerator)
            .thenConsumeWhile(x -> x >= 0)
            .expectComplete()
            .verify();
}
```

In the preceding test case, the following has occurred:

- thenConsumeWhile has been configured with the x >= 0 predicate. This should match all values except the first negative value.
- Next, we expect a complete event and then verify it using the verify API. This is shown in the following screenshot:

We have looked at the `expect` methods to validate events generated in a Reactive Stream. If the expectation does not match, `StepVerifier` builds a generic message to indicate the failure. `StepVerifier` also provides support to build failure-specific and descriptive messages. `StepVerifier` provides the `as` method, which can be invoked after the `expect` method. The `as` method takes a string, which is displayed when the exception does not match:

```
@Test
  public void testExpectationWithDescp() throws Exception {
      // removed for brevity
      StepVerifier.create(fibonacciGenerator.take(9))
              .expectNext(0L, 1L, 1L).as("Received 0,1,1 numbers")
              .expectNextCount(7).as("Received 9 numbers")
              .expectComplete()
              .verify();
  }
```

In this code, we have provided descriptive messages for each expectation. If the expectation does not match, the test fails with a specific error message, as shown in the following trace. This helps in debugging test failures:

```
java.lang.AssertionError: expectation "Received 9 numbers" failed
(expected: count = 7; actual: counted = 6; signal: onComplete())

    at
reactor.test.DefaultStepVerifierBuilder.failPrefix(DefaultStepVerifierBuild
er.java:2235)
    at
reactor.test.DefaultStepVerifierBuilder.fail(DefaultStepVerifierBuilder.jav
a:2231)
```

Capture values

There are times when we are unable to assert values directly. In such test scenarios, we usually capture the invoked values and then assert them separately. Reactor provides a `recordWith` API to capture values generated by the publisher under test. This method takes a `Supplier` function, which is invoked in order to instantiate a Collection for storing values. The recorder collection can then be asserted using the `expectRecordedMatches` method:

```
@Test
    public void testRecordWith() throws Exception {
        Flux<Long> fibonacciGenerator = Flux.generate(() -> Tuples.<Long,
                Long>of(0L, 1L), (state, sink) -> {
        //    Removed for Brevity
```

```
        });
        StepVerifier.create(fibonacciGenerator, Long.MAX_VALUE)
                .recordWith(() -> new ArrayList<>())
                .thenConsumeWhile(x -> x >= 0)
                .expectRecordedMatches(x -> x.size() > 0)
                .expectComplete()
                .verify();
    }
```

In the preceding code, we have done the following:

1. Configured `recordWith` to use an `ArrayList` for recording all values.
2. Configured `thenConsumeWhile` with the predicate `x >= 0`. This should match all values except the first negative value. All matching values are added to the record collection.
3. Next, we configured `expectRecordedMatches` to assert the record collection to have values.
4. Finally, we expect a completion event and then verify it using the `verify` API as follows:

When running the preceding test case, we should get a green bar for passing tests. This is shown in the following screenshot:

As well as the `expectRecordWith` method, Reactor also provides a `consumeRecordWith` API, which can be invoked for custom assertions. The `consumeRecordWith` method takes a Consumer function for the recorded collection. It is important to note that a recorded session can only be matched with the next `consumeRecordWith` or `expectRecordWith` invocation.

Verify

As discussed previously, the `verify` operator is used to assert the configured behavior. The termination event for a publisher must be validated before the `verify` call. Alternatively, Reactor provides convenient verify methods to validate the termination event and assert the complete configured chain. Similar to `expectError`, the API is offered in the following methods:

Method name	Description
`verifyComplete()`	This method only validates the occurrence of a completion event.
`verifyError()`	This method only validates the occurrence of an error event.
`verifyError(exceptionClass)`	This method validates an error event and matches an underlying exception class wrapped in the error event.
`verifyError(exceptionMsg)`	This method validates an error event and matches an underlying exception message wrapped in the error event.
`verifyError(predicate)`	This method validates an error event and matches it against the supplied predicate.
`verfiyErrorSatisfies(assertConsumer)`	This method validates an error event and matches the underlying exception for supplied custom assertions.

In the preceding test, we can replace `expectComplete` and verify invocations with the following snippet:

```
StepVerifier.create(fibonacciGenerator.take(10))
        .expectNext(0L,  1L,  1L)
        .expectNextCount(7)
        .verifyComplete();
```

We will leave the test execution to the reader. Again, a passed test should show a green bar. It is important to note that `verify` (and related methods) return `Duration`. The duration specifies the actual time the test took to execute. This also brings us to discussing the blocking behavior of verify methods. By default, the invocation of verify methods is synchronous and blocking. It can make the test wait infinitely. The behavior can be changed by specifying a `Duration` in the `verify` method call. Alternatively, we can set a default timeout by using the `StepVerifier.setDefaultTimeout` method:

```
@Test
    public void testWithTimeout() throws Exception {
        Flux<Long> fibonacciGenerator = Flux.generate(() -> Tuples.<Long,
            // removed for brevity
        });
StepVerifier.create(fibonacciGenerator.take(9).delaySequence(Duration.ofSec
onds(1)))
                .expectNext(0L,  1L,  1L)
                .expectNextCount(7)
                .expectComplete()
```

```
                    .verify(Duration.ofMillis(100));
    }
```

In this code, we have made the following changes:

- Delayed event generation for 1 second by using the `delaySequence` operator.
- Removed the `verifyComplete` call, as we cannot specify a duration. Instead, we added the `expectComplete` method call.
- Lastly, we used the verify call with a timeout duration. The timeout is set to 100 milliseconds.

This test case times out and fails with the following exception:

```
java.lang.AssertionError: VerifySubscriber timed out on
reactor.core.publisher.SerializedSubscriber@1a57272

    at
reactor.test.DefaultStepVerifierBuilder$DefaultVerifySubscriber.pollTaskEve
ntOrComplete(DefaultStepVerifierBuilder.java:1522)
    at
reactor.test.DefaultStepVerifierBuilder$DefaultVerifySubscriber.verify(Defa
ultStepVerifierBuilder.java:1107)
    at
reactor.test.DefaultStepVerifierBuilder$DefaultStepVerifier.verify(DefaultS
tepVerifierBuilder.java:729)
    at ReactorTest.testWithTimeout(ReactorTest.java:58)
```

In the previous sections, we looked at methods that enable us to validate most of the operators for a Reactive Stream. We will cover some specific Reactor scenarios next.

Validating backpressure

As discussed previously in `Chapter` 7, *Flow Control and Backpressure*, backpressure allows a subscriber to control event flow. This mechanism is aimed at controlling a fast generating producer. There are different configurations for backpressure. These configurations have already been discussed in `Chapter` 7, *Flow Control and Backpressure*, and we will not cover them here. Fundamentally, backpressure skips delivering values to the Subscriber. Consequently, validating it means that we must look for values that have not been delivered to the Subscriber. Reactor provides the `verifyThenAssertThat` API for the same reason. This method exposes assertions that can validate the end state of a publisher. Let's now work with a test case:

```
@Test
public void testBackPressure() throws Exception {
```

```
Flux<Integer> numberGenerator = Flux.create(x -> {
    System.out.println("Requested Events :" +
x.requestedFromDownstream());
    int number = 1;
    while (number < 100) {
        x.next(number);
        number++;
    }
    x.complete();
}, FluxSink.OverflowStrategy.ERROR);

StepVerifier.create(numberGenerator, 1L)
        .thenConsumeWhile(x -> x >= 0)
        .expectError()
        .verifyThenAssertThat()
        .hasDroppedElements();
}
```

In the preceding code, the following occurred:

1. We configured a Publisher with `OverflowStrategy.ERROR` using the `Flux.create` API. Our Publisher generates 100 events without looking for more requests from the Subscriber.

2. Next, our `StepVerifier` is configured for only one event, limiting the request rate from the Subscriber. This is achieved using the `StepVerifier.create` API.

3. Since the subscriber is asking for one event and the Publisher is raising 100 events, this should lead to a backpressure error. In the test case, we configured `expectError()` to validate the error raised.

4. Lastly, we configured `verfiyThenAssertThat()` to check for dropped elements.

The preceding test case validates the complete scenario of backpressure, which is shown in the following screenshot:

In the preceding test case, we have validated whether or not elements have been dropped. Reactor also provides the following assertions to validate various other scenarios:

Method name	Description
hasDroppedElements	This method verifies whether or not elements have been dropped by a Publisher due to overflow.
hasNotDroppedElements	This method verifies whether or not any elements have been dropped by a Publisher due to overflow.
hasDroppedExactly	This method validates the dropped values against the ones supplied in the method invocation.
hasDroppedErrors	This method verifies whether or not errors have been dropped by a Publisher.
hasOperatorErrors	This method verifies whether or not operator errors have been raised by stream processing.

Validating time operations

Validating time-based operations is a complex task. Traditionally, we used `Thread.sleep` or `wait-notify` blocks to simulate the delay in the test case. Reactor also provides rich support to validate such operations. This allows us to build a virtual clock by using the `Stepverifier.withVirtualTime` method for Reactive Streams. The virtual clock can then be manipulated using any of the following operations to simulate time drift for the required operation:

Operations	Description
thenAwait	This only pauses the execution for the configured time.
expectNoEvent	This pauses the execution and validates that no event has happened during the configured delay.

It is important to note that operators must be invoked after injecting the virtual clock. Also, the `expectNoEvent` API recognizes subscription as an event. If it is used as the first step after injecting the virtual clock, then it will fail due to the Subscription event. Let's now work with the following test case:

```
@Test
 public void testDelay() {
     StepVerifier.withVirtualTime(() -> Flux.just(1, 2, 3, 4, 5, 6, 7, 8, 9)
                  .delaySequence(Duration.ofMillis(100)))
              .expectSubscription()
              .thenAwait(Duration.ofSeconds(100))
              .expectNextCount(9)
              .verifyComplete();
     }
```

In the preceding code, we achieved the following:

1. Created a Flux with the virtual clock using `StepVerifier.withVirtualTime`
2. Configured a `delaySequence` operation on the Reactive Stream
3. Invoked `thenAwait` to hold the virtual clock for the configured time
4. Expected nine values to be published, followed by a completion event

Let's now run the test case and verify it as follows:

Publisher probe

In the preceding section, we used `StepVerifier` to assert the steps executed in a reactive chain. However, these are often simple chains that can be validated end-to-end in a single test case. There may be scenarios where we need to inject a Publisher into a service or a method and verify the published signals. In such cases, we can instrument an existing Publisher using the `PublisherProbe` utility. The probe keeps track of signals published by the Publisher. In the end, we can assert and verify the final state of the probe. The utility helps to unit test a service or method executing some specific logic on a Reactive Publisher.

A `PublisherProbe` can be constructed using either of the following methods:

- `PublisherProbe.Of(ExisitingPublisher)`: Instruments an existing Publisher and generates a probe from it. The probe sends out signals as generated by the original Publisher.
- `PublisherProbe.empty()`: Creates an empty sequence probe. This probe does not emit any signals.

We can get back a Mono or Flux from the `PublisherProbe` by invoking respective methods. The Flux/Mono can then be passed to the method/service under test. After the invocation, the final state can be verified using the following assertions:

Method name	Description
assertWasSubscribed	This method validates that the Publisher was subscribed to in the invocation.
assertWasRequested	This method validates that the Publisher was requested in the invocation.
assertWasCancelled	This method validates that the Publisher was cancelled in the invocation.

The following code depicts this:

```
@Test
public void testPublisherProbe() throws Exception {
    Flux<Long> fibonacciGenerator = Flux.generate(() -> Tuples.<Long,
            Long>of(0L, 1L), (state, sink) -> {
        if (state.getT1() < 0)
            sink.complete();
        else
            sink.next(state.getT1());
        return Tuples.of(state.getT2(), state.getT1() + state.getT2());
    });

    PublisherProbe<Long> publisherProbe =
PublisherProbe.of(fibonacciGenerator);
    publisherProbe.flux().subscribe();

    publisherProbe.assertWasSubscribed();
    publisherProbe.assertWasRequested();

}
```

In the preceding code, we have done the following:

1. Created a `PublisherProbe` using `fibonacciGenerator`
2. Next we subscribed to the Flux generated by the probe
3. In the end we validate that the Flux was subscribed, flowed by the request event

Let's run the test case and verify it as follows:

Publisher stubs

So far, we have been creating a `Publisher` along with the operators. As a result, we could build end-to-end validations. However, in most business services, a `Publisher` will be created in some part of the code and operations will be performed in another. In order to unit test the operation service code, we would need to generate a dummy `Publisher`. Reactor also provides `TestPublisher` for this purpose. We can create a `TestPublisher` using the `create factory` method. The generated `TestPublisher` can be converted into a Flux or a Mono. `TestPublisher` makes it possible to emit events using any of the following methods:

Method name	Description
`next(T) / next(T,T...)`	Invokes Publisher OnNext with the supplied values.
`complete()`	Terminates the Publisher stream with the OnComplete event.
`error()`	Terminates the Publisher stream with the OnError event.
`emit(T,T,T .....)`	Invokes Publisher OnNext with the supplied values, followed by OnComplete termination.

Let's work with sample code. We have the following `PrintService`, which prints even numbers to the console as follows:

```
class PrintService{
    public void printEventNumbers(Flux<Long> source, PrintWriter writer) {
        source
                .filter(x -> x % 2 == 0)
                .subscribe(writer::println);
    }
}
```

Now, let's build a simple test case. In the test case, we will inject a few values and a `StringWriter`. At the end, we will validate whether or not `StringWriter` contains all the required values, as follows:

```
@Test
public void testPublisherStub() throws Exception {
    TestPublisher<Long> numberGenerator= TestPublisher.<Long>create();
    StringWriter out = new StringWriter();
    new PrintService().printEventNumbers(numberGenerator.flux(),
     new PrintWriter(out));
    numberGenerator.next(1L,2L,3L,4L);
    numberGenerator.complete();
    assertTrue(out.getBuffer().length() >0);
}
```

In the preceding code, we have done the following:

1. Generated a `TestPublisher` using the `create` method
2. Instantiated a `StringWriter` to capture printed values
3. Next, we generated `onNext` using some values
4. Finally, we generated `onComplete` and validated the printed values

Now, run the test case. This should show a green bar for a test that has passed:

`TestPublisher` also keeps track of the final state of the `Publisher` stub. The final state can be verified using the following assertions:

assertSubscribers	This method validates that the Publisher was subscribed to by the number of subscribers supplied in the invocation.
assertCancelled	This method validates that the Publisher was canceled multiple times, as specified by the number supplied in the invocation.
assertRequestOverflow	This method validates that the Publisher raised Overflow conditions by generating more events than asked for by the subscriber.

In the preceding test case, we built a well-behaved `Publisher` stub. This did not send null events or raise more events than requested. The `TestPublisher` utility also enables us to instantiate Publisher, which violates the preceding conditions. Such a Publisher can be used to validate service/operator behaviors. An inconsistent Publisher can be generated using the `createNonCompliant` method. This method uses a violation type and generates configured errors:

```
@Test
public void testNonCompliantPublisherStub() throws Exception {
    TestPublisher<Long> numberGenerator=
TestPublisher.createNoncompliant(TestPublisher.Violation.REQUEST_OVERFLOW);
    StepVerifier.create(numberGenerator, 1L)
            .then(() -> numberGenerator.emit(1L,2L,3L,4L))
            .expectNext(1L)
            .verifyError();

}
```

In the preceding code, we have done the following:

1. Generated a `TestPublisher` using the `createNonCompliant` method. Publisher has been configured to produce more than the requested events.
2. Subscribed to the publisher with an initial demand of one element.
3. Validated the produced element followed by an error termination.

Debugging Reactor streams

Debugging Rector streams is not straightforward. This is due to the fact that all stream processing in Reactor is asynchronous and non-blocking. In a synchronous and blocking system, an error stacktrace points to the root cause of the issue. However, in an asynchronous reactor stream, the error is logged in the `Subscriber` but has been raised in an operator in stream processing. The error stacktrace does not mention the operator. Let's take a look at the following Reactor stacktrace:

```
reactor.core.Exceptions$ErrorCallbackNotImplemented:
java.lang.IllegalStateException

Caused by: java.lang.IllegalStateException
    at ReactorDebug.lambda$testPublisherStub$1(ReactorDebug.java:22)
    at
reactor.core.publisher.FluxGenerate$GenerateSubscription.fastPath(FluxGener
ate.java:223)
    at
```

```
reactor.core.publisher.FluxGenerate$GenerateSubscription.request(FluxGenera
te.java:202)
    at
reactor.core.publisher.FluxFilterFuseable$FilterFuseableSubscriber.request(
FluxFilterFuseable.java:170)
    at
reactor.core.publisher.LambdaSubscriber.onSubscribe(LambdaSubscriber.java:8
9)
    at
reactor.core.publisher.FluxFilterFuseable$FilterFuseableSubscriber.onSubscr
ibe(FluxFilterFuseable.java:79)
    at reactor.core.publisher.FluxGenerate.subscribe(FluxGenerate.java:83)
    at
reactor.core.publisher.FluxFilterFuseable.subscribe(FluxFilterFuseable.java
:51)
    at reactor.core.publisher.Flux.subscribe(Flux.java:6877)
    at reactor.core.publisher.Flux.subscribeWith(Flux.java:7044)
    at reactor.core.publisher.Flux.subscribe(Flux.java:6870)
    at reactor.core.publisher.Flux.subscribe(Flux.java:6834)
    at reactor.core.publisher.Flux.subscribe(Flux.java:6777)
    at PrintService.printEventNumbers(ReactorProbe.java:57)
    at ReactorDebug.testPublisherStub(ReactorDebug.java:28)
    at sun.reflect.NativeMethodAccessorImpl.invoke0(Native Method)
    at
sun.reflect.NativeMethodAccessorImpl.invoke(NativeMethodAccessorImpl.java:6
2)
    at
sun.reflect.DelegatingMethodAccessorImpl.invoke(DelegatingMethodAccessorImp
l.java:43)
    at java.lang.reflect.Method.invoke(Method.java:498)
    at
org.junit.runners.model.FrameworkMethod$1.runReflectiveCall(FrameworkMethod
.java:50)
    at
org.junit.internal.runners.model.ReflectiveCallable.run(ReflectiveCallable.
java:12)
    at
org.junit.runners.model.FrameworkMethod.invokeExplosively(FrameworkMethod.j
ava:47)
```

In the preceding stacktrace, we can observe the following:

- `IllegalStateException` has reached our subscriber
- Reactor also raises an `ErrorCallbackNotImpletemented`, since the Subscriber does not handle the error event
- The error is captured while performing `PrintService.printEventNumbers`
- The preceding error is raised in our `ReactorDebug.testPublisherStub` test case

This does not help much, but we can clean up the stack trace by first implementing an error handler. The simplest approach here is to use the `printstackTrace` method of throwable:

```
class PrintService{
    public void printEventNumbers(Flux<Long> source, PrintWriter writer) {
        source
                .filter(x -> x % 2 == 0)
                .subscribe(writer::println,Throwable::printStackTrace);
    }
}
```

The preceding change to the `subscribe` method sanitizes the stacktrace of the error raised. However, the error operator is still not explained in the trace, as shown in the following code:

```
java.lang.IllegalStateException
    at ReactorDebug.lambda$testPublisherStub$1(ReactorDebug.java:22)
    at
reactor.core.publisher.FluxGenerate$GenerateSubscription.fastPath(FluxGener
ate.java:223)
    at
reactor.core.publisher.FluxGenerate$GenerateSubscription.request(FluxGenera
te.java:202)
    at
reactor.core.publisher.FluxFilterFuseable$FilterFuseableSubscriber.request(
FluxFilterFuseable.java:170)
    at
reactor.core.publisher.LambdaSubscriber.onSubscribe(LambdaSubscriber.java:8
9)
    at
reactor.core.publisher.FluxFilterFuseable$FilterFuseableSubscriber.onSubscr
ibe(FluxFilterFuseable.java:79)
    at reactor.core.publisher.FluxGenerate.subscribe(FluxGenerate.java:83)
    at
reactor.core.publisher.FluxFilterFuseable.subscribe(FluxFilterFuseable.java
:51)
    at reactor.core.publisher.Flux.subscribe(Flux.java:6877)
```

```
    at reactor.core.publisher.Flux.subscribeWith(Flux.java:7044)
    at reactor.core.publisher.Flux.subscribe(Flux.java:6870)
    at reactor.core.publisher.Flux.subscribe(Flux.java:6834)
    at reactor.core.publisher.Flux.subscribe(Flux.java:6804)
    at PrintService.printEventNumbers(ReactorProbe.java:57)
    at ReactorDebug.testPublisherStub(ReactorDebug.java:28)
    ........
    ......
    at
com.intellij.rt.execution.junit.IdeaTestRunner$Repeater.startRunnerWithArgs
(IdeaTestRunner.java:47)
    at
com.intellij.rt.execution.junit.JUnitStarter.prepareStreamsAndStart(JUnitSt
arter.java:242)
    at
com.intellij.rt.execution.junit.JUnitStarter.main(JUnitStarter.java:70)
```

Debug hook

Reactor provides assembly-time instrumentation capability to debug a stacktrace. This
capability enables us to intercept all invocations of Flux/Mono operations. Each interception
then keeps a record of the error thrown with the operation invoked. The resultant mapping
is then appended to the stacktrace. This record can then be used to find the root cause of the
issue. Since this is an additional interception, which keeps a record mapping, it should only
be invoked to debug errors and must not be enabled in production systems. Reactor
provides a `Hooks.OnOperatorDebug` API, which must be invoked before instantiating the
Flux/Mono. Let's invoke `Hooks.OnOperatorDebug` in our test case, as follows:

```
    @Test
    public void testPublisherStub() throws Exception {
        Hooks.onOperatorDebug();
        Flux<Long> fibonacciGenerator = getFibonacciGenerator();
        StringWriter out = new StringWriter();
        new PrintService().printEventNumbers(fibonacciGenerator,new
PrintWriter(out));
        assertTrue(out.getBuffer().length() >0);
    }
class PrintService {
    public void printEventNumbers(Flux<Long> source, PrintWriter writer) {
        source
                .filter(x -> x % 2 == 0)
                .subscribe(writer::println,Throwable::printStackTrace);
    }
}
```

Let's run our test case and look at the generated stacktrace, which is as follows:

```
java.lang.IllegalStateException
    at ReactorDebug.lambda$getFibonacciGenerator$1(ReactorDebug.java:30)
    at
reactor.core.publisher.FluxGenerate$GenerateSubscription.fastPath(FluxGener
ate.java:223)
    at
reactor.core.publisher.FluxGenerate$GenerateSubscription.request(FluxGenera
te.java:202)
    ..........
    at
com.intellij.rt.execution.junit.JUnitStarter.main(JUnitStarter.java:70)
    Suppressed: reactor.core.publisher.FluxOnAssembly$OnAssemblyException:
Assembly trace from producer [reactor.core.publisher.FluxGenerate] :
    reactor.core.publisher.Flux.generate(Flux.java:947)
    ReactorDebug.getFibonacciGenerator(ReactorDebug.java:27)
    ReactorDebug.testPublisherStub(ReactorDebug.java:19)
Error has been observed by the following operator(s):
    |_   Flux.generate(ReactorDebug.java:27)
    |_   Flux.filter(ReactorProbe.java:58)
```

Now, if we look at the bottom of the trace, it clearly states that an error has been thrown in the `Flux.generate` invocation. To solve this, we can fix this bug and rerun our test case.

Checkpoint operator

The Debug hook discussed in the previous section has a global impact, instrumenting all Flux/Mono instances. Consequently, the impact of the debug hook is application-wide. Alternatively, Reactor also provides a `checkpoint` operator, which can only alter a particular Flux stream. The `checkpoint` operator instruments a Reactor Streams after the operator invocation. We can alter our previous test case as follows:

```
@Test
public void testPublisherStub() throws Exception {
  Flux<Long> fibonacciGenerator =
    getFibonacciGenerator().checkpoint();
    StringWriter out = new StringWriter();
  new PrintService().printEventNumbers(fibonacciGenerator,
   new PrintWriter(out));
  assertTrue(out.getBuffer().length() >0);
}
```

In the preceding code, we have invoked the `checkpoint()` operator after creating the Flux. The modified test case generates the following stacktrace. Since the `checkpoint` operator is invoked after `Flux.generate`, the record mapping refers to `FluxGenerate` as the point of error. This is shown with the following code:

```
java.lang.IllegalStateException
    at ReactorDebug.lambda$getFibonacciGenerator$1(ReactorDebug.java:29)
    at
reactor.core.publisher.FluxGenerate$GenerateSubscription.fastPath(FluxGener
ate.java:223)
    at
reactor.core.publisher.FluxGenerate$GenerateSubscription.request(FluxGenera
te.java:202)
    ..........
    at
com.intellij.rt.execution.junit.JUnitStarter.prepareStreamsAndStart(JUnitSt
arter.java:242)
    at
com.intellij.rt.execution.junit.JUnitStarter.main(JUnitStarter.java:70)
    Suppressed: reactor.core.publisher.FluxOnAssembly$OnAssemblyException:
Assembly trace from producer [reactor.core.publisher.FluxGenerate] :
    reactor.core.publisher.Flux.checkpoint(Flux.java:2690)
    reactor.core.publisher.Flux.checkpoint(Flux.java:2640)
    ReactorDebug.testPublisherStub(ReactorDebug.java:18)
Error has been observed by the following operator(s):
    |_  Flux.checkpoint(ReactorDebug.java:18)
```

The `checkpoint` and the `debug` operators discussed previously have an impact on the memory footprint of the application. Both these operators try to save stacktraces, which leads to higher memory consumption. Due to this, these operators cannot be enabled in production applications without paying an additional cost. But the `checkpoint` operator also offers a trimmed down version, which does not save any stacktraces. The `checkpoint` operator, when configured with a description message, disables stacktrace accumulation. The following stacktrace is generated when using checkpoint with a description in our preceding code:

```
java.lang.IllegalStateException
    at ReactorDebug.lambda$getFibonacciGenerator$1(ReactorDebug.java:29)
    at
reactor.core.publisher.FluxGenerate$GenerateSubscription.fastPath(FluxGener
ate.java:223)
    .......
    at
com.intellij.junit4.JUnit4IdeaTestRunner.startRunnerWithArgs(JUnit4IdeaTest
Runner.java:68)
    at
```

```
com.intellij.rt.execution.junit.IdeaTestRunner$Repeater.startRunnerWithArgs
(IdeaTestRunner.java:47)
    at
com.intellij.rt.execution.junit.JUnitStarter.prepareStreamsAndStart(JUnitSt
arter.java:242)
    at
com.intellij.rt.execution.junit.JUnitStarter.main(JUnitStarter.java:70)
    Suppressed: reactor.core.publisher.FluxOnAssembly$OnAssemblyException:
Assembly site of producer [reactor.core.publisher.FluxGenerate] is
identified by light checkpoint [generator check]."description" : "generator
check"
```

In the preceding stacktrace, Reactor used the description and prefixed the `identified by light checkpoint` message to it. It no longer tries to build a stacktrace of operator invocations. The `identified by light checkpoint` message can be in searched in application logs. But if the description message is not good enough, Reactor allows us to enable stacktrace capturing in order to build informative failure traces. This can be accomplished by using the `checkpoint(description, enableStackTrace)` operator.

Stream logging

Logging is one of the most common ways to know what is happening underneath method invocations. Reactor uses SLF4J for logging, but it does not log stream operations out-of-the-box. Instead, Reactor provides the `log` operator, which can be used to selectively enable logging for a particular stream. Let's modify our test case using the log operator as follows:

```
@Test
public void testPublisherStub() throws Exception {
  Flux<Long> fibonacciGenerator = getFibonacciGenerator().log();
  StringWriter out = new StringWriter();
  new PrintService().printEventNumbers(fibonacciGenerator,
   new PrintWriter(out));
  assertTrue(out.getBuffer().length() >0);
}
```

The `log()` operator is offered in many variants. By default, the operator logs at the `INFO` level. We can configure this to log at the `DEBUG` or other levels as well. Furthermore, we can also place a `logback.xml` file to format the logged message, as follows:

```
<configuration>
    <appender name="stdout" class="ch.qos.logback.core.ConsoleAppender">
        <encoder>
            <pattern>
                %d{HH:mm:ss.SSS} [%thread] [%-5level] %logger{36} - %msg%n
```

```
            </pattern>
          </encoder>
      </appender>
    <root level="DEBUG">
          <appender-ref ref="stdout"/>
      </root>
  </configuration>
```

In the preceding `logback.xml` file, we have configured a `stdout` appender. The appender will be invoked in a synchronous and blocking manner. Reactor also provides a `reactor-logback` library, which can be used to log messages in an asynchronous manner. The preceding test case now generates the following log message:

```
23:07:09.139 [main] [DEBUG] reactor.util.Loggers$LoggerFactory - Using
Slf4j logging frameworkthe
23:07:09.419 [main] [INFO ] reactor.Flux.Generate.1 - |
onSubscribe([Fuseable] FluxGenerate.GenerateSubscription)
23:07:09.450 [main] [INFO ] reactor.Flux.Generate.1 - | request(unbounded)
23:07:09.462 [main] [INFO ] reactor.Flux.Generate.1 - | onNext(0)
23:07:09.463 [main] [INFO ] reactor.Flux.Generate.1 - | onNext(1)
23:07:09.471 [main] [INFO ] reactor.Flux.Generate.1 - | request(1)
........
23:07:09.958 [main] [INFO ] reactor.Flux.Generate.1 - | request(1)
23:07:10.087 [main] [ERROR] reactor.Flux.Generate.1 - |
onError(java.lang.IllegalStateException)
23:07:10.126 [main] [ERROR] reactor.Flux.Generate.1 -
java.lang.IllegalStateException: null
    at ReactorDebug.lambda$getFibonacciGenerator$1(ReactorDebug.java:29)
    at
reactor.core.publisher.FluxGenerate$GenerateSubscription.fastPath(FluxGener
ate.java:223)
    at
reactor.core.publisher.FluxGenerate$GenerateSubscription.request(FluxGenera
te.java:202)
    at ..........
```

The preceding logging output clearly shows what events are happening in stream processing. We can interpret the log and build the following analysis:

1. Each log line outputs the operator invoked. Consequently, we can see that the first subscription was raised.
2. Next, there was an unbounded request, which started generating events.
3. After that, the Subscriber raised a request for one element.
4. Finally, there was an `ERROR` event invoked in the generate operator due to `IllegalStateException`.

Consequently, we can see that logging is a powerful mechanism for debugging and learning more about application stream processing.

Summary

This chapter focused on testing and debugging Reactor Streams. Testing Reactor Flux/Mono streams is complex, as each stream is evaluated lazily in an async manner. We also looked at `StepVerifier`, which can validate individual steps in isolation. Next, we looked at a virtual clock to validate time-sensitive operations, such as delays. We also looked at the `PublisherProbe` utility used to validate a Publisher's end state. Then, in order to unit test Reactive operators and stream business logic, we performed stubbing using `TestPublisher`. The next section was about debugging Reactor Streams to gain further knowledge about under-the-covers processing. Debugging Reactor streams is complex, since the operators are evaluated in an asynchronous manner. We looked at the Debug hook and checkpoint operator to generate an operator mapped error stacktrace. Finally, we looked at the log operator used to generate logs for stream processing.

We have also come to the end of our book. On this journey, we learned about Reactor, an implementation of the Reactive Streams specification. We worked with Flux and Mono Publishers. We built simple applications to find out more about the available operators. We came to the conclusion that Reactor is a library that can be used in any Java application.

On this journey, we also discussed SpringWebFlux, a complete web framework using Rector. We developed simple web services using it and explored the backpressure behavior offered by Reactor. We concluded the journey by looking at various advanced features of Reactor.

Questions

1. Which test utility class is available in Reactor to validate the invoked operations on a stream?
2. What is the difference between `PublisherProbe` and `TestPublisher`?
3. How should the virtual clock be configured to validate time-bound operations?
4. What is the difference between the `onOperatorDebug` hook and the checkpoint operator?
5. How can we turn on logging for stream processing?

Assessments

Chapter 1: Getting Started with Reactive Streams

1. What are the principles of the Reactive Manifesto?

   The Reactive Manifesto defines the following principles:

   - **Message-Driven**: All application components should be loosely coupled and communicate using messages
   - **Responsive**: An application must respond to user input in a timely manner
   - **Resilient**: An application must isolate failures to individual components
   - **Scalable**: An application must react to changes in workload

2. What are Reactive Extensions?

   Reactive Extensions are libraries in imperative languages that enables us to write asynchronous, event-driven reactive applications. The libraries enable us to express asynchronous events as a set of observables. This enables us to build application components that can receive and process these async events. On the other hand, there are also event producers, which push these events.

3. What does the Reactive Streams specification cater to?

   Reactive Streams is a specification that determines the minimum set of interfaces required to build the asynchronous processing of a large volume of unbounded data. It is a specification aimed at JVM and JavaScript runtime. The main goal of the Reactive Streams specification is to standardize the exchange of stream data across an asynchronous boundary of applications.

4. What are the principles upon which Reactive Streams are based?

Reactive Streams are based on the following two principles:

- **Asynchronous execution**: This is the ability to execute tasks without having to wait for previously executed tasks to finish first. The execution model decouples tasks so that each of them can be performed simultaneously, utilizing the available hardware.
- **Backpressure**: A subscriber can control events in its queue to avoid any overruns. It can also request more events if there is additional capacity.

5. What are the salient features of the Reactor Framework?

- **Infinite data streams**: This refers to Reactor's capability of generating infinite sequences of data.
- **Push-pull model**: In Reactor, a producer can push events. On the other hand, if the consumer is slow in processing, it can pull events at its own rate.
- **Concurrency agnostic**: Reactor does not enforce any concurrency model. It allows a developer to select what fits best.
- **Operator vocabulary**: Reactor provides a wide range of operators. These operators allow us to select, filter, transform, and combine streams.

Chapter 2: The Publisher and Subscriber APIs in a Reactor

1. How can we validate Reactive Streams publisher and subscriber implementations?

In order to validate a publisher, the Reactive Streams API has published a test compatibility kit called `reactive-streams-tck`. Reactive publisher can be verified using the `PublisherVerifier` interface. Similarly, a subscriber can be verified by using the `SubscriberBlackboxVerification<T>` abstract class.

2. How is the Reactive Streams publisher-subscriber model different from the JMS API?

In JMS, the producer is responsible for generating unbounded events on the queue or topics, while the consumer actively consumes the events. The producer and consumer are working in isolation, at their own rates. The task of managing the subscription is taken care of by the JMS broker. There is no concept of backpressure in JMS. Also, it lacks event modeling, such as subscription, error, or completion.

3. How is the Reactive Streams publisher-subscriber model different from the Observer API?

   The Observable API has the responsibility of determining a change and publishing it to all interested parties. The API is about entity state changes. This is not what we are modeling with the `Publisher` and `Subscriber` interface. The `Publisher` interface is responsible for generating unbounded events. The `Subscriber`, on the other hand, lists all kinds of events, such as data, error, and completion.

4. What is the difference between Flux and Mono?

   `Flux` is a general-purpose reactive publisher. It represents a stream of asynchronous events with zero or more values. On the other hand, Mono can only generate a maximum of one event.

5. What is the difference between `SynchronousSink` and `FluxSink`?

   `SynchronousSink` can generate only one event at a time. It is synchronous in nature. A subscriber must consume the event before generating the next event. On the other hand, `FluxSink` can generate many events asynchronously. Moreover, it does not take subscription cancelation or backpressure into account. This means that even if the subscriber has canceled its subscription, the `create` API will continue to generate events.

6. What are the different lifecycle hooks available in Reactor?

- `doOnSubscribe`: For the subscribe event
- `doOnRequest`: For the request event
- `doOnNext`: For the next event
- `doOnCancel`: For the subscription cancel event
- `doOnError`: For an error event
- `doOnCompletion`: For completion event

- doOnTerminate: For termination due to error, completion, or cancelation
- doFinally: For clean-up post termination of a stream
- doOnEach: For all events

Chapter 3: Data and Stream Processing

1. Which operator is used to select data elements from a stream?

- filter
- filterWhen
- take
- takeLast
- last
- distinct
- single
- elementAT

2. Which operator is used to reject data elements from a stream?

- filter
- filterWhen
- skip
- skipLast
- SkipUntil
- ignoreElements

3. Which operators does Reactor offer for data conversion? How are these operators different from each other?

- map: This is used for one-to-one transformation
- flatMap: This is used for one-to-n transformation

4. How can we perform data aggregation by using Reactor operators?

- collectList
- collectMap
- collectMultiMap

5. Which conditional operators are offered by Reactor?

-   `all`: Represents the AND operator
-   `any`: Represents the OR operator

Chapter 4: Processors

1. What are the limitations of `DirectProcessor`?

    `DirectProcessor` does not offer any backpressure handling.

2. What are the limitations of `UnicastProcessor`?

    `UnicastProcessor` can work with only a single subscriber.

3. What are the capabilities of `EmitterProcessor`?

    `EmitterProcessor` is a processor that can be used with several subscribers. Multiple subscribers can ask the processor for the next value event, based on their individual rates of consumption

4. What are the capabilities of `ReplayProcessor`?

    `ReplayProcessor` is a special-purpose processor, capable of caching and replaying events to its subscribers.

5. What are the capabilities of `TopicProcessor`?

    `TopicProcessor` is a processor capable of working with multiple subscribers, using an event-loop architecture. The processor delivers events from a publisher to the attached subscribers in an asynchronous manner and honors backpressure for each subscriber by using the RingBuffer data structure.

6. What are the capabilities of `WorkQueueProcessor`?

    `WorkQueueProcessor` can connect to multiple subscribers. It does not deliver all events to each subscriber. The demand from every subscriber is added to a queue and events from a publisher are sent to any of the subscribers.

7. What is the difference between a hot publisher and a cold publisher?

Cold publishers have an individual subscription state for each subscriber. They publish all data to each of the subscribers irrespective of the subscription time. On the other hand, a hot publisher publishes common data to all its subscribers. Thus, new subscribers get only the current events and no older events are delivered to them.

Chapter 5: SpringWebFlux for Microservices

1. How can we configure the `SpringWebFlux` project?

`SpringWebFlux` can be configured in two ways :

- **Using annotations**: `SpringWebFlux` supports `SpringWebMVC` annotations. This is the easiest way of configuring `SpringWebFlux`.
- **Using functional endpoints**: This model allows us to build Java 8 functions as web endpoints. The application can be configured as a set of routes, handlers, and filters.

2. Which `MethodParameter` annotations are supported by `SpringWebFlux`?

- `@PathVariable`: This annotation is used to access values for URI template variables
- `@RequestParam`: This annotation is used to determine values passed as query parameters
- `@RequestHeader`: This annotation is used to determine values passed in request headers
- `@RequestBody`: This annotation is used to determine values passed in the request body
- `@CookieValue`: This annotation is used to determine HTTP cookie values as part of request
- `@ModelAttribute`: This annotation is used to determine an attribute from the request model or instantiate one if not present
- `@SessionAttribute`: This annotation is used to determine preexisting session attributes
- `@RequestAttribute`: This annotation is used to determine preexisting request attributes created by a previous filter execution

3. What is the use of `ExceptionHandler`?

`SpringWebFlux` supports exception handling by creating methods that are annotated with `@ExceptionHandler`.

4. What is the use of `HandlerFunction` ?

`SpringWebFlux` handler function is responsible for serving a given request. It takes the request in the form of a `ServerRequest` class and generates the response as `ServerResponse`.

5. What is the use of `RouterFunction` ?

`SpringWebFlux` router function is responsible for routing incoming requests to the correct handler function.

6. What is the use of `HandlerFilter` ?

`HandlerFilter` is analogous to the Servlet filter. This executes before the request gets processed by `HandlerFunction`. There could be chain filters, which get executed before the request gets served.

Chapter 6: Dynamic Rendering

1. How does the `SpringWebFlux` framework resolve a View?

The framework invokes `ViewResolutionResultHandler` using the `HandlerResult` returned for the endpoint invocation. `ViewResolutionResultHandler` then determines the correct view by validating the returned value for the following:

- **String**: If the returned value is a string, then the framework builds a view using the configured `ViewResolvers`
- **Void**: If nothing is returned, it then tries to build the default view
- **Map**: The framework looks for the default view but it also adds the key values returned into the request model

`ViewResolutionResultHandler` looks up the content type passed in the request. In order to determine which view should be used, it compares the content type passed to the content type supported by `ViewResolver`. It then selects the first `ViewResolver`, which supports the request content type.

2. Which components need to be configured so you can use the Thymeleaf template engine?

- Add `spring-boot-starter-thymeleaf` to the project
- Create an instance of `ThymeleafReactiveViewResolver`
- Add the resolver to `ViewResolverRegistry`, available in the `configureViewResolvers` method

3. Which API is used to configure static resources in SpringWebFlux?

- The `addResourceHandler` method takes a URL pattern and configures it to be a static location
- The `addResourceLocations` method configures a location from where the static content needs to be served

4. What are the benefits of `WebClient`?

`WebClient` is a non-blocking, asynchronous HTTP client for making requests. It can be configured with Java 8 lambdas for processing data.

5. What is the difference between the retrieve and exchange APIs of WebClient?

- `Retrieve`: This can decode a request body into a Flux or Mono
- `Exchange`: The `Exchange` method provides the complete message, which can be converted back into a target type

Chapter 7: Flow Control and Backpressure

1. Why do we need the `groupBy` operator?

The `groupBy()` operator converts `Flux<T>` into batches. The operator associates a key with each element of `Flux<T>`. It then groups elements that have the same key. These groups are then emitted by the operator.

2. What is the difference between the `groupBy` and `buffer` operators?

The `groupBy` operator groups the stream of events based on a configured key, but the `buffer` operator splits the stream into chunks of a specified size. Thus, the `buffer` operator maintains the original ordering of events.

3. How can we throttle an event in Reactor?

   The `sample()` operator allows us to accomplish throttling.

4. What is the difference between the `Overflow.Ignore` and the `OverFlow.Latest` strategies?

   `Overflow.Ignore` ignores the limits of the subscriber backpressure and keeps delivering the next event to the subscriber. `OverFlow.Latest` keeps the latest event raised in the buffer. The subscriber will only get the latest produced event when the next request is raised.

5. Which operators are available for changing the backpressure strategy of a producer?

   - `onBackpressureDrop()`
   - `onBackpressureLatest()`
   - `onBackpressureError()`
   - `onBackpressureBuffer()`

Chapter 8: Handling Errors

1. How is an error handled in Reactor?

   Errors arise when either the publisher or the subscriber throws back an exception. Reactor intercepts the exception, builds an `Error` event, and then sends it to the subscriber. The subscriber must implement `ErrorCallbackHandler` to handle the error.

2. Which operators allow us to configure error handling?

   - `onErrorReturn`
   - `onErrorResume`
   - `onErrorMap`

3. What is the difference between `onErrorResume` and `onErrorReturn`?

   The `OnErrorReturn` operator provides a fall-back value in the event of an error. On the other hand, the `OnErrorResume` operator provides a fall-back value stream instead of a single fall-back value.

4. How can we generate a timely response for a Reactive Streams?

The `timeout()` operator can be configured for a time interval. The operator will raise an error when it first discovers a delay of more than the configured time. The operator also has a fallback Flux. The fallback value is returned once the timeout expires.

5. How does the `retry` operator behave?

The `retry` operator allows us to resubscribe to a published stream when an error is discovered. The `retry` operation can only be performed a fixed number of times. The resubscribed events are handled as next events by the subscriber. If the stream completes normally, no next retry takes place.

Chapter 9: Execution Control

1. What are the different types of schedulers available in Reactor?

- `Schedulers.immediate`: This schedules on the current thread
- `Schedulers.single`: This schedules on a single thread
- `Schedulers.parallel`: This schedules on the thread pool
- `Schedulers.elastic`: This schedules on a thread pool
- `Schedulers.fromExecutor`: This schedules the configured executor service

2. Which scheduler should be used for blocking operations?

`Schedulers.elastic` schedules on a thread pool.

3. Which scheduler should be used for computation intensive operations?

- `Schedulers.single`: This schedules on a single thread.
- `Schedulers.parallel`: This schedules on the thread pool

4. How are `PublishOn` and `SubscriberOn` different from each other?

The `subscribeOn` operator intercepts events from a publisher in the execution chain and sends them to a different scheduler for the complete chain. It is important to note that the operator changes the execution context for the complete chain, unlike the `publishOn` operator, which only alters the execution of a downstream chain.

5. What is the limitation of `ParallelFlux`?

    `ParallelFlux` does not offer the `doFinally` lifecycle hook. It can be converted back to a `Flux` using the `sequential` operator, which can then be configured using the `doFinally` hook.

6. Which operators are available for generating a `ConnectedFlux`?

- `replay`
- `publish`

Chapter 10: Testing and Debugging

1. Which test utility class is available in Reactor to validate the invoked operations on a stream?

    Reactor provides the `StepVerifier` component to validate the required operations in isolation.

2. What is the difference between `PublisherProbe` and `TestPublisher`?

    The `PublisherProbe` utility can instrument an existing publisher. The probe keeps track of signals published by the publisher, which can be validated at the end of the test. On the other hand, `TestPublisher` is capable of generating the `Publisher` stub, which can be used to unit test Reactor operators.

3. How should the virtual clock be configured to validate time-bound operations ?

    The virtual clock must be injected before performing any time-based operations.

4. What is the difference between the `onOperatorDebug` hook and the `checkpoint` operator?

    The `onOperatorDebug` hook makes a global change for all reactive pipelines. On the other hand, the `checkpoint` operator makes the change specific to the stream it is applied to.

5. How can we turn on the logging of stream processing?

    The `log` operator can be used to turn on logging.

Other Books You May Enjoy

If you enjoyed this book, you may be interested in these other books by Packt:

Scala Reactive Programming
Rambabu Posa

ISBN: 9781787288645

- Understand the fundamental principles of Reactive and Functional programming
- Develop applications utilizing features of the Akka framework
- Explore techniques to integrate Scala, Akka, and Play together
- Learn about Reactive Streams with real-time use cases
- Develop Reactive Web Applications with Play, Scala, Akka, and Akka Streams
- Develop and deploy Reactive microservices using the Lagom framework and ConductR

Reactive Programming with Swift 4
Navdeep Singh

ISBN: 9781787120211

- Understand the practical benefits of Rx on a mobile platform
- Explore the building blocks of Rx, and Rx data flows with marble diagrams
- Learn how to convert an existing code base into RxSwift code base
- Learn how to debug and test your Rx Code
- Work with Playgrounds to transform sequences by filtering them using map, flatmap and other operators
- Learn how to combine different operators to work with Events in a more controlled manner.
- Discover RxCocoa and convert your simple UI elements to Reactive components
- Build a complete RxSwift app using MVVM as design pattern

Leave a review - let other readers know what you think

Please share your thoughts on this book with others by leaving a review on the site that you bought it from. If you purchased the book from Amazon, please leave us an honest review on this book's Amazon page. This is vital so that other potential readers can see and use your unbiased opinion to make purchasing decisions, we can understand what our customers think about our products, and our authors can see your feedback on the title that they have worked with Packt to create. It will only take a few minutes of your time, but is valuable to other potential customers, our authors, and Packt. Thank you!

Index

V

view resolution
  about 106
  map 106
  string 106
  void 106
view templates
  about 105

freemarker 107, 109
scripting 116
Thymeleaf 111, 114
view resolution 106

W

WebClient 123, 164, 166, 167
window operator 134, 135, 136